Spanish
phrase book

AA Publishing

Contents

English edition prepared by First Edition Translations Ltd, Great Britain

Designed and produced by AA Publishing

Distributed in the United Kingdom by AA Publishing, Norfolk House, Priestley Road, Basingstoke, Hampshire RG24 9NY

First published in 1995 as Wat & Hoe Spaans, © Uitgeverij Kosmos bv - Utrecht/Antwerpen

Van Dale Lexicografie bv - Utrecht/Antwerpen

This edition © The Automobile Association 1997

Reprinted 1997

A CIP catalogue record for this book is available from the British Library

ISBN: 0 7495 1477 9

Published by AA Publishing (a trading name of Automobile Association Developments Limited, whose registered office is Norfolk House, Priestley Road, Basingstoke, Hampshire RG24 9NY. Registered number 1878835).

Typeset by Anton Graphics Ltd, Andover, Hampshire.

Printed and bound by G. Canale C.SpA, Torino, Italy.

Cover photographs: Oranges, Majorca, AA Photo Library (P. Baker); Flamenco dancer, Jerez, Powerstock Photo Library; Sagrada Familia, Barcelona, Powerstock Photo Library

Introduction

● **Welcome to the AA's new Essential Phrase Books series, covering the most popular European languages and containing everything you'd expect from a comprehensive language series. They're concise, accessible and easy to understand, and you'll find them indispensable on your trip abroad.**

Each guide is divided into 15 themed sections and starts with a pronunciation table which explains the phonetic pronunciation to all the words and phrases you'll need to know for your trip, while at the back of the book is an extensive word list and grammar guide which will help you construct basic sentences in your chosen language.

Throughout the book you'll come across coloured boxes with a 🌑 beside them. These are designed to help you if you can't understand what your listener is saying to you. Hand the book over to them and encourage them to point to the appropriate answer to the question you are asking.

Other coloured boxes in the book – this time without the symbol – give alphabetical listings of themed words with their English translations beside them.

For extra clarity, we have put all English words and phrases in black, foreign language terms in red and their phonetic pronunciation in italic.

This phrase book covers all subjects you are likely to come across during the course of your visit, from reserving a room for the night to ordering food and drink at a restaurant and what to do if your car breaks down or you lose your traveller's cheques and money. With over 2,000 commonly used words and essential phrases at your fingertips you can rest assured that you will be able to get by in all situations, so let the Essential Phrase Book become your passport to a secure and enjoyable trip!

Pronunciation table

The pronunciation provided should be read as if it were English, bearing in mind the following main points:

Vowels

Vowels in Spanish are very open

a	is like a in amber,	*ah*	as in **casa**	*kahsah*
e	is like e in egg,	*eh*	as in **esta**	*ehstah*
i	is like ee in seen,	*ee*	as in **isla**	*eeslah*
o	is like o in John,	*oh*	as in **hotel**	*ohtehl*
u	is like oo in room,	*oo*	as in **uno**	*oonoh*
y	is like ee in seen,	*ee*	as in **y**	*ee*
	the diphthong **ay** is pronounced as in aisle or eye			
			as in **hay**	*eye*

Consonants

Consonants are as in English, pronounced less clearly, except

b/v	are pronounced roughly the same		
		as in **vamos**	*bahmohs*
c	before e and i is soft and is like the **th** in **th**atch		
		as in **la acera**	*lah ahthehrah*
	before a,o and u is hard		
		as in **cosa**	*kohsah*
cu	before another vowel is pronounced like **cw**		
		as in **la cuenta**	*lah kwehntah*
g	before e and i is soft and is like the Scottish **ch** in lo**ch**,		
		as in **la gente**	*lah hehnteh*
	before a, o and u is hard		
		as in **gato**	*ghahtoh*
gu	before e and i is pronounced as hard **g**		
		as in **la guía**	*geeah*
	before a, o and u is pronounced like **gw**		
		as in **guapo**	*gwahpoh*
gü	before e and i is pronounced like **gw**		
		as in **lingüística**	*leengwees-teekah*
h	is silent		
j	is like the soft **g**	as in **jarra**	*hahrrah*
ll	is like **lli** in billion	as in **llave**	*lyahbeh*
ñ	is like **ni** in onion	as in **año**	*ahnyoh*
r	is rolled as in the Scottish **r**, **rr** is a longer roll		
z	is like **th** in **th**ought	as in **taza**	*tahthah*

The stress normally falls on the last syllable of the word (**hotel**), except that words ending in a vowel (not including **y**) or in n or s (**casa, casas**) are stressed on the next to the last syllable. All exceptions are indicated by a written acute accent (**Córdoba**, *kohrdohbah*).

Note: In the south, the soft **c** and the **z** are pronounced *s*. This is also true in Latin America.

1

Useful lists

Useful lists

1.1 **T**oday or tomorrow?

What day is it today?	¿Qué día es hoy? *keh deeah ehs oy?*
Today's Monday	Hoy es lunes *oy ehs loonehs*
– Tuesday	Hoy es martes *oy ehs mahrtehs*
– Wednesday	Hoy es miércoles *oy ehs myehrkohlehs*
– Thursday	Hoy es jueves *oy ehs <u>h</u>ooehbehs*
– Friday	Hoy es viernes *oy ehs byehrnehs*
– Saturday	Hoy es sábado *oy ehs sahbahdoh*
– Sunday	Hoy es domingo *oy ehs dohmeengoh*
in January	en enero *ehn ehnehroh*
since February	desde febrero *dehsdeh fehbrehroh*
in spring	en primavera *ehn preemahbehrah*
in summer	en verano *ehn behrahnoh*
in autumn	en otoño *ehn ohtohnyoh*
in winter	en invierno *ehn eenbyehrno*
1997	mil novecientos noventa y siete *meel nohbehthyentohs nohbehntah ee syehteh*
the twentieth century	el siglo XX (veinte) *ehl seegloh beheenteh*
What's the date today?	¿Qué día es hoy? *keh deeah ehs oy?*
Today's the 24th	Hoy es 24 (veinticuatro) *oy ehs beheenteekwahtroh*
Monday 3 November 1998	lunes 3 (tres) de noviembre de 1998 (mil novecientos noventa y ocho) *loonehs trehs deh nohbyehmbreh deh meel nohbehthyehntohs nohbehntah ee ohchoh*
in the morning	por la mañana *pohr lah mahnyahnah*
in the afternoon	por la tarde *pohr lah tahrdeh*
in the evening	por la noche *pohr lah nohcheh*
at night	por la noche *pohr lah nohcheh*
this morning	esta mañana *ehstah mahnyahnah*

this afternoon _____	esta tarde
	ehstah tahrdeh
this evening _____	esta noche
	ehstah nohcheh
tonight _____	esta noche
	ehstah nohcheh
last night _____	anoche
	ahnohcheh
this week _____	esta semana
	ehstah sehmahnah
next month _____	el mes próximo
	ehl mehs prohxeemoh
last year _____	el año pasado
	ehl ahnyo pahsahdoh
next... _____	el/la... próximo/a
	ehl/lah... prohxeemoh/ah
in...days/weeks/ _____	dentro de...días/semanas/meses/años
months/years	*dehntroh deh...*
	deeahs/sehmahnahs/mehsehs/ahnyohs
...weeks ago _____	hace...semanas
	ahthe...sehmahnahs
day off _____	día libre
	deeah leebreh

🕐 .2 Bank Holidays

● **The most important** Bank Holidays in Spain are the following:

January 1	New Year's Day (Año Nuevo)
January 6	Epiphany (Epifanía)
March 19	St. Joseph's Day (San José)
March/April	Good Friday (Viernes Santo)
March/April	Easter Monday(Catalonia) (Lunes Santo)
May 1	Labour Day (Día del Trabajo)
May/June	Corpus Christi (Corpus Christi)
July 25	St. James's Day (Santiago)
August 15	Assumption Day (Asunción)
October 12	Columbus Day (Día de las Américas)
November 1	All Saints' Day (Todos los Santos)
December 6	Constitution Day (Día de la Constitución)
December 8	Immaculate Conception (Inmaculada Concepción)
December 25	Christmas (Navidad)

There are also various regional holidays like San Fermín in Pamplona (July 6-13) and the Fallas in Valencia (March 19).

🕐 .3 What time is it?

What time is it? _____	¿Qué hora es?
	keh ohrah ehs?
It's nine o'clock _____	Son las nueve
	sohn lahs nwehbeh
– five past ten _____	Son las diez y cinco
	sohn lahs dyeth ee theenkoh
– a quarter past eleven ____	Son las once y cuarto
	sohn lahs ohntheh ee kwahrtoh
– twenty past twelve _____	Son las doce y veinte
	sohn lahs dohthe ee beheenteh

– half past one _____	Es la una y media	
	ehs lah oonah ee mehdyah	
– twenty–five to three_____	Son las tres menos veinticinco	
	sohn lahs trehs mehnohs	
	beheenteetheenkoh	
– a quarter to four _____	Son las cuatro menos cuarto	
	sohn lahs kwahtroh mehnohs kwahrtoh	
– ten to five _____	Son las cinco menos diez	
	sohn lahs theenkoh mehnohs dyehth	
– twelve noon_____	Son las doce del mediodía	
	sohn lahs dohtheh dehl mehdyohdeeah	
– midnight _____	Son las doce de la noche	
	sohn lahs dohtheh deh lah nohcheh	

half an hour _____	media hora	
	mehdyah ohrah	
What time? _____	¿A qué hora?	
	ah keh ohrah?	
What time can I come _____	¿A qué hora puedo pasar?	
round?	*ah keh ohrah pwehdoh pahsahr?*	
At... _____	A las...	
	ah lahs...	
After... _____	Después de las...	
	dehspwehs deh lahs...	
Before... _____	Antes de las...	
	ahntehs deh lahs...	
Between...and... _____	Entre las...y las...	
	ehntreh lahs...ee lahs...	
From...to... _____	De las...a las...	
	deh lahs...ah lahs...	
In...minutes _____	Dentro de...minutos	
	dehntroh deh...meenootohs	
– an hour _____	Dentro de una hora	
	dehntroh deh oonah ohrah	
– ...hours _____	Dentro de...horas	
	dehntroh deh...ohrahs	
– a quarter of an hour ____	Dentro de un cuarto de hora	
	dehntroh deh oon kwahrtoh deh ohrah	
– three quarters of_____	Dentro de tres cuartos de hora	
an hour	*dehntroh deh trehs kwahrtohs deh ohrah*	

early/late _____	muy temprano/tarde	
	mwee tehmprahnoh/tahrdeh	
on time _____	a tiempo	
	ah tyehmpoh	
summer opening hours____	horario de verano	
	ohrahryoh deh behrahnoh	
winter opening hours_____	horario de invierno	
	ohrahryoh deh eenbyehrnoh	

1 .4 One, two, three...

0 _____	cero	*thehroh*
1 _____	uno	*oonoh*
2 _____	dos	*dohs*
3 _____	tres	*trehs*
4 _____	cuatro	*kwahtroh*

5 _____	cinco	*theenkoh*
6 _____	seis	*sehees*
7 _____	siete	*syehteh*
8 _____	ocho	*ohchoh*
9 _____	nueve	*nwehbeh*
10 _____	diez	*dyeth*
11 _____	once	*ohntheh*
12 _____	doce	*dohtheh*
13 _____	trece	*trehtheh*
14 _____	catorce	*kahtohrtheh*
15 _____	quince	*keentheh*
16 _____	dieciséis	*dyetheesehees*
17 _____	diecisiete	*dyetheesyehteh*
18 _____	dieciocho	*dyetheeohchoh*
19 _____	diecinueve	*dyetheenwehbe*
20 _____	veinte	*beheenteh*
21 _____	veintiuno	*beheenteeoonoh*
22 _____	veintidós	*beheenteheedohs*
30 _____	treinta	*treheentah*
31 _____	treinta y uno	*treheentah ee oonoh*
32 _____	treinta y dos	*treheentah ee dohs*
40 _____	cuarenta	*kwahrehntah*
50 _____	cincuenta	*theenkwehntah*
60 _____	sesenta	*sehsehntah*
70 _____	setenta	*sehtehntah*
80 _____	ochenta	*ohchehntah*
90 _____	noventa	*nohvehntah*
100 _____	cien	*thyehn*
101 _____	ciento uno	*thyehntoh oonoh*
110 _____	ciento diez	*thyehntoh dyeth*
120 _____	ciento veinte	*thyehntoh beheenteh*
200 _____	doscientos	*dohsthyehntohs*
300 _____	trescientos	*trehsthyehntohs*
400 _____	cuatrocientos	*kwahtrohthyehntohs*
500 _____	quinientos	*keenyehntohs*
600 _____	seiscientos	*seheesthyehntohs*
700 _____	setecientos	*sehtehthyehntohs*
800 _____	ochocientos	*ohchohthyehntohs*
900 _____	novecientos	*nohbehthyentohs*
1000 _____	mil	*meel*
1100 _____	mil cien	*meel thyehn*
2000 _____	dos mil	*dohs meel*
10,000 _____	diez mil	*dyeth meel*
100,000 _____	cien mil	*thyehn meel*
1,000,000 _____	un millón	*oon meelyohn*
1st _____	primero	*preemehroh*
2nd _____	segundo	*sehgoondoh*
3rd _____	tercero	*tehrthehroh*
4th _____	cuarto	*kwahrtoh*
5th _____	quinto	*keentoh*
6th _____	sexto	*sehxtoh*
7th _____	séptimo	*sehpteemoh*
8th _____	octavo	*ohktahboh*

9th	noveno	*nohvehnoh*
10th	décimo	*dehtheemoh*
11th	undécimo	*oondehtheemoh*
12th	duodécimo	*doo-ohdehtheemo*
13th	decimotercero	*dehtheemohtehrthehroh*
14th	decimocuarto	*dehtheemohkwahrtoh*
15th	decimoquinto	*dehtheemohkeentoh*
16th	decimosexto	*dehtheemohsehxtoh*
17th	decimoséptimo	*dehtheemosehpteemoh*
18th	decimoctavo	*dehtheemohktahboh*
19th	decimonoveno	*dehtheemonobenoh*
20th	vigésimo	*beeheseemoh*
21st	vigesimoprimero	*beeheseemohpreemeroh*
22nd	vigesimosegundo	*beeheseemohsegoondoh*
30th	trigésimo	*treeheseemoh*
100th	centésimo	*thentehseemoh*
1,000th	milésimo	*meelehseemoh*

once	una vez
	oonah behth
twice	dos veces
	dos behthes
double	el doble
	ehl dohbleh
triple	el triple
	ehl treepleh
half	la mitad
	lah meetath
a quarter	un cuarto
	oon kwartoh
a third	un tercio
	oon terthyoh
a couple, a few, some	unos, algunos
	oonohs, algoonohs

2 + 4 = 6	dos más cuatro, seis
	dohs mahs kwahtroh, sehees
4 – 2 = 2	cuatro menos dos, dos
	kwahtroh mehnohs dohs, dohs
2 x 4 = 8	dos por cuatro, ocho
	dohs pohr kwahtroh, ohchoh
4 ÷ 2 = 2	cuatro dividido dos, dos
	kwahtroh deebeedeedoh dohs, dohs

odd/even	par/impar
	pahr/eempahr
total	(en) total
	(ehn) tohtahl
6 x 9	seis por nueve
	sehees pohr nwehbeh

① .5 The weather

Is the weather going to be good/bad?	¿Hará buen/mal tiempo?
	ahrah bwehn/mahl tyehmpoh?
Is it going to get colder/hotter?	¿Hará más frío/calor?
	ahrah mahs freeoh/kahlohr?

Useful lists

What temperature is it going to be?	¿Cuántos grados hará? *kwahntohs grahdohs ahrah?*
Is it going to rain?	¿Va a llover? *bah ah lyohbehr?*
Is there going to be a storm?	¿Tendremos tormenta? *tehndrehmohs tohrmehntah?*
Is it going to snow?	¿Va a nevar? *bah ah nehbahr?*
Is it going to freeze?	¿Va a helar? *bah ah ehlahr?*
Is the thaw setting in?	¿Comenzará el deshielo? *kohmehnzahrah ehl dehsyeloh*
Is it going to be foggy?	¿Habrá niebla? *ahbrah nyehblah?*
Is there going to be a thunderstorm?	¿Habrá tormenta eléctrica? *ahbrah tohrmehntah ehlehktreekah?*
The weather's changing	Va a cambiar el tiempo *bah ah kahmbyahr ehl tyehmpoh*
It's cooling down	Va a refrescar *bah ah rehfrehskahr*
What's the weather going to be like today/tomorrow?	¿Qué tiempo hará hoy/mañana? *keh tyehmpoh ahrah oy/mahnyahnah?*

algo nublado/nublado	granizo	ola de calor
light/heavy clouds	hail	heat wave
bochornoso	...grados(bajo/sobre cero)	pesado
stormy	...degrees(above/below zero)	muggy
bueno	helada	sofocante
fine	(black) ice	scorching hot
caluroso	húmedo	soleado
hot	damp	sunny
chubasco	huracán	suave
shower	hurricane	mild
cielo cubierto	llovizna	tormenta eléctrica
overcast	drizzle	thunderstorm
desapacible	lluvia	vendaval
bleak	rain	gale
despejado	lluvioso	ventoso
clear	wet	windy
escarcha	niebla	viento
frost	fog	wind
fresco	nieve	viento leve /moderado/ fuerte
chilly	snow	light/moderate/ strong wind
frlo	nublado	tempestad
cold	cloudy	squall

Useful lists

See also 5.1 Asking for directions

here/there	aquí/allá
	ahkee/ahlyah
somewhere/nowhere	en alguna/ninguna parte
	ehn algoonah/neengoonah pahrteh
everywhere	en todas partes
	ehn tohdahs pahrtehs
far away/nearby	lejos/cerca
	lehhos/thehrkah
right/left	a la derecha/izquierda
	ah lah dehrehchah/eethkyehrdah
to the right/left of	a la derecha/izquierda de
	ah lah dehrehchah/eethkyehrdah deh
straight ahead	todo recto
	tohdoh rehktoh
via	pasando por
	pahsahndoh pohr
in	en
	ehn
on	sobre
	sohbreh
under	debajo de
	dehbahhoh deh
against	contra
	kohntrah
opposite	frente a
	frehnteh ah
next to	al lado de
	ahl lahdoh deh
near	junto a
	hoontoh ah
in front of	delante de
	dehlahnteh deh
in the centre	en el medio
	ehn ehl mehdyoh
forward	hacia adelante
	ahthyah ahdehlanteh
down	(hacia) abajo
	(ahthyah) ahbahhoh
up	(hacia) arriba
	(ahthya) ahrreebah
inside	(hacia) adentro
	(ahthya) ahdehntroh
outside	(hacia) afuera
	(ahthya) ahfwehrah
behind	(hacia) atrás
	(ahthya) ahtrahs
at the front	delante
	dehlahnteh
at the back	detrás
	dehtrahs
in the north	en el norte
	ehn ehl nohrteh

to the south _____	hacia el sur
	ahthya ehl soor
from the west _____	del oeste
	dehl ohehsteh
from the east _____	del este
	dehl ehsteh
...of _____	al...de
	ahl...deh

.7 What does that sign say?

See 5.4 Traffic signs

abierto/cerrado	horario (de apertura)	prohibido pisar el
open/closed	opening hours	césped
agua no potable	información	keep off the grass
no drinking water	information	razón aquí
alta tensión	liquidación (por	inquiries
high voltage	cese)	rebajas
ascensor	closing-down sale	clearance
lift	no funciona	recepción
caballeros	out of order	reception
gents/gentlemen	no tocar	recién pintado
caja	please do not touch	wet paint
pay here	peligro	reservado
completo	danger	reserved
full	peligro de incendio	saldos
coto privado	fire hazard	sale
private (property)	...piso	salida
cuidado con el perro	...floor	exit
beware of the dog	primeros auxilios	salida de
cuidado, escalón	first aid	emergencia/salida
mind the step	prohibido el paso	de socorro
entrada	no entry	emergency exit
entrance	prohibido fotografiar	se alquila
entrada libre	no photographs	for hire
free admission	prohibido fumar	se ruega no molestar
escalera	no smoking	do not disturb
stairs	prohibido hacer	se vende
escalera de	fuego	for sale
incendios	no open fires	señoras
fire escape	prohibido para	ladies
escalera mecánica	animales	servicios
escalator	no pets allowed	toilets
freno de emergencia		empujar/tirar
emergency brake		push/pull

.8 Telephone alphabet

a _____ *ah*	de Antonio	*deh ahntohnyoh*
b _____ *beh*	de Barcelona	*deh bahr-thehlohnah*
c _____ *theh*	de Carmen	*deh kahrmehn*
ch _____ *cheh*	de chocolate	*deh choh kohlahteh*
d _____ *deh*	de Dolores	*deh dohlohrehs*

15

e	_eh_	de Enrique	_deh ehnreekeh_
f	_hefeh_	de Francia	_deh frahnthyah_
g	_heh_	de Gerona	_de hehrohnah_
h	_ahcheh_	de historia	_de eestohryah_
I	_ee_	de Inés	_deh eenehs_
j	_hohtah_	de José	_deh hohseh_
k	_kah_	de Kilo	_deh keeloh_
l	_ehleh_	de Lorenzo	_deh lohrehnthoh_
ll	_ehlyeh_	de Llobregat	_deh lyohbrehgaht_
m	_ehmeh_	de Madrid	_deh Mahdreedh_
n	_ehneh_	de Navarra	_deh nahbahrrah_
ñ	_ehnyeh_	de ñoño	_deh nyohnyoh_
o	_oh_	de Oviedo	_deh ohbyedoh_
p	_peh_	de París	_deh pahrees_
q	_koo_	de querido	_deh kehreedoh_
r	_ehrreh_	de Ramón	_deh rahmohn_
s	_ehseh_	de sábado	_deh sahbahdoh_
t	_teh_	de Tarragona	_deh tahrrahgohnah_
u	_oo_	de Ulises	_deh ooleesehs_
v	_oobeh_	de Valencia	_deh bahlehnthyah_
w	_oobehdohbleh_	de Washington	_deh wahsheengtohn_
x	_ehkees_	de Xiquena	_deh heekehnah_
y	_eegryehgah_	griega	
z	_thehtah_	de Zaragoza	_deh thahrahgohthah_

1 .9 Personal details

surname	apellidos
	ahpehlyeedohs
christian name(s)	nombre
	nohmbreh
initials	iniciales
	eeneethyahlehs
address (street/number)	dirección (calle/número)
	deerehkthyohn (kahlyeh/noomehroh)
post code/town	código postal/población
	cohdeegoh pohstahl/pohblahthyon)
sex (male/female)	sexo (v = varón, m = mujer)
	sehksoh (v = bahrohn, m = moohehr)
nationality	nacionalidad
	nahthyohnahleeedah
date of birth	fecha de nacimiento
	fehchah deh nahteemyehntoh
place of birth	lugar de nacimiento
	loogahr deh natheemyehntoh
occupation	profesión
	profehsyohn
married/single/divorced	casado, casada/soltero, soltera/ divorciado, divorciada
	kahsahdoh, kahsahdah/sohltehroh, sohltehrah/deebohrthyahdoh, deebohrthyahdah
widowed	viuda/viudo
	byoodah/byoodoh
(number of) children	(número de) hijos
	(noomehroh deh) eehohs

| passport/identity card/driving licence/ number, place and date of issue | pasaporte/carnet de identidad/permiso de conducir/número, lugar y fecha de expedición |
| | *kahrneh deh eedehnteedahdh (pahsahpohrteh/pehrmeesoh deh kohndootheer) noomehroh, loogahr ee fehchah deh ehkspehdeethyohn* |

Courtesies

2 Courtesies

● **Female friends and relatives** kiss on both cheeks in Spain. In shops, etc., you will hear *¡Buenos días!* or just *¡Buenas!*, and expect to be addressed in Basque or Catalan in these provinces. For example you will hear *¡Agur!* instead of *¡Adiós!* in the Basque Country.

2.1 Greetings

Hello, Mr Smith	Hola, buenos días *ohlah, bwehnohs deeahs*
Hello, Peter	Hola, Pedro *ohlah, pehdroh*
Hi, Helen	Qué hay, Elena *keh ay, ehlehnah*
Good morning, madam	Buenos días, señora (before 2pm) *bwehnohs deeahs, sehnyohrah*
Good afternoon, sir	Buenas tardes, señor (after 2pm) *bwehnahs tahrdehs, sehnyohr*
Good evening	Buenas tardes (before 9pm), buenas noches (after 9pm) *bwehnahs tahrdehs, bwehnahs nohchehs*
How are you?	¿Qué tal? *keh tahl?*
Fine, thank you, and you?	Muy bien, ¿y usted? *mwee byehn, ee oostehdh?*
Very well	Estupendo *ehstoopehndoh*
Not very well	Regular *rehgoolahr*
Not too bad	Tirando *teerando*
I'd better be going	Bueno, me voy *bwehnoh, meh boy*
I have to be going. Someone's waiting for me	Tengo que irme. Me están esperando *tehngoh keh eermeh, meh ehstahn ehspehrahndoh*
Bye!	¡Adiós! *ahdyohs!*
Goodbye	Hasta luego *ahstah lwehgoh*
See you soon	Hasta pronto *ahstah prohntoh*
See you later	Hasta luego *ahstah lwehgoh*
See you in a little while	Hasta ahora *ahstah ahohrah*
Sleep well	Que descanse *keh dehskahnseh*
Good night	Buenas noches *bwehnahs nohchehs*
All the best	Que le vaya bien *keh leh bahyah byehn*
Have fun	Que se divierta, que lo pase bien *keh seh deebyehrtah, keh loh pahseh byehn*

Good luck	Mucha suerte
	moochah swehrteh
Have a nice holiday	Felices vacaciones
	fehleethehs bahkahthyohnehs
Have a good trip	Buen viaje
	bwehn byahheh
Thank you, you too	Gracias, igualmente
	grahthyahs, eegwahlmehnteh
Say hello to...for me	Recuerdos a...
	rehkwehrdohs ah...

2 .2 How to ask a question

Who?	¿Quién?
	kyehn?
Who's that?	¿Quién es?
	kyehn ehs?
What?	¿Qué?
	keh?
What's there to see here?	¿Qué se puede visitar aquí?
	keh seh pwehdeh beeseetahr ahkee?
What kind of hotel is that?	¿Qué clase de hotel es?
	keh klahseh deh ohtehl ehs?
Where?	¿Dónde?
	dohndeh?
Where's the toilet?	¿Dónde están los servicios?
	dohndeh ehstahn lohs sehrbeethyohs?
Where are you going?	¿A dónde va?
	ahdohndeh bah?
Where are you from?	¿De dónde es usted?
	deh dohndeh ehs oostehdh?
How?	¿Cómo?
	kohmoh?
How far is that?	¿A qué distancia queda?
	ah keh deestahnthyah kehdah?
How long does it take?	¿Cuánto dura?
	kwahntoh doorah?
How long is the trip?	¿Cuánto dura el viaje?
	kwahntoh doorah ehl byahheh?
How much?	¿Cuánto?
	kwahntoh?
How much is this?	¿Cuánto vale?
	kwahntoh bahleh?
What time is it?	¿Qué hora es?
	keh ohrah ehs?
Which?	¿Cuál? ¿Cuáles?
	kwahl? kwahlehs?
Which glass is mine?	¿Cuál es mi copa?
	kwahl ehs mee kohpah?
When?	¿Cuándo?
	kwahndoh?
When are you leaving?	¿Cuándo sale?
	kwahndoh sahleh?
Why?	¿Por qué?
	pohr keh?
Could you...me?	¿Podría...?
	pohdreeah...?

Could you help me, please?	¿Podría ayudarme? *pohdreeah ahyoodahrmeh?*
Could you point that out to me?	¿Me lo podría indicar? *meh loh pohdreeah eendeekahr?*
Could you come with me, please?	¿Le importaría acompañarme? *leh eempohrtahreeah ahkohmpahnyahrmeh?*
Could you...	¿Quiere...?/¿Podría...? *kyereh...?/pohdreeah...?*
Could you reserve some tickets for me, please?	¿Me podría reservar entradas? *meh pohdreeah rehsehrbahr ehntrahdahs?*
Do you know...?	¿Sabe...? *sahbeh...?*
Do you know another hotel, please?	¿Sabría indicarme otro hotel? *sahbreeah eendeekahrmeh ohtroh ohtehl?*
Do you know whether...?	¿Tiene...? *tyehneh...?*
Do you have a...?	¿Me podría dar un(a)...? *meh pohdreeah dahr oon(ah)...?*
Do you have a vegetarian dish, please?	¿Tendría un plato sin carne? *tehndreeah oon plahtoh seen kahrneh?*
I'd like...	Quisiera... *keesyehrah...*
I'd like a kilo of apples, please.	Quisiera un kilo de manzanas *keesyehrah oon keeloh deh mahnthahnahs*
Can I...?	¿Puedo...?/¿Se puede...? *pwehdoh...?/seh pwehdeh?*
Can I take this?	¿Podría llevármelo? *pohdreeah lyehbahrmehloh?*
Can I smoke here?	¿Se puede fumar aquí? *seh pwehdeh foomahr ahkee?*
Could I ask you something?	¿Puedo hacerle una pregunta? *pwehdoh ahthehrleh oonah prehgoontah?*

2 .3 How to reply

Yes, of course	Sí, claro *see, klahroh*
No, I'm sorry	No, lo siento *noh, loh syehntoh*
Yes, what can I do for you?	Sí. ¿En qué puedo servirle? *see, ehn keh pwehdoh sehrbeerleh?*
Just a moment, please	Un momento, por favor *oon mohmehntoh, pohr fahbohr*
No, I don't have time now	No, ahora no tengo tiempo *noh, aohrah noh tehngoh tyehmpoh*
No, that's impossible	No, eso es imposible *noh, ehsoh ehs eempohseebleh*
I think so	Creo que sí *krehoh keh see*
I agree	Yo también lo creo *yoh tahmbyehn loh krehoh*
I hope so too	Yo también lo espero *yoh tahmbyehn loh ehspehroh*
No, not at all	No, de ninguna manera *noh, deh neengoonah mahnehrah*
No, no-one	No, nadie *noh, nahdyeh*

No, nothing _____	No, nada *noh, nahdah*
That's (not) right _____	(No) es cierto *(noh) ehs thyehrtoh*
I (don't) agree _____	(No) estoy de acuerdo con usted *(noh) ehstoy deh ahkwehrdoh kohn oostehdh*
All right _____	Está bien *ehstah byehn*
Okay _____	Vale *bahleh*
Perhaps _____	Quizá *keethah*
I don't know _____	No lo sé *noh loh seh*

2 .4 Thank you

Thank you _____	Gracias *grahthyahs*
You're welcome _____	De nada *deh nahdah*
Thank you very much _____	Muchísimas gracias *moocheeseemahs grahthyahs*
Very kind of you _____	Muy amable (de su parte) *mwee ahmahbleh (deh soo pahrteh)*
I enjoyed it very much _____	Ha sido un verdadero placer *ah seedoh oon behrdahdehroh plahthehr*
Thank you for your _____ trouble	Gracias por la molestia *grahthyahs pohr lah mohlehstyah*
You shouldn't have _____	No se hubiera molestado *noh seh oobyehrah mohlehstahdoh*
That's all right _____	No se preocupe *noh seh prehohkoopeh*

2 .5 Sorry

Excuse me _____	Perdone *pehrdohneh*
Sorry! _____	¡Perdone! *pehrdohneh!*
I'm sorry, I didn't know... ___	Perdone, no sabía que... *pehrdohneh, noh sahbeeah keh...*
I do apologise _____	Perdone *pehrdohneh*
I'm sorry _____	Lo siento *loh syehntoh*
I didn't do it on purpose, ___ it was an accident	No ha sido a propósito; ha sido sin querer *noh ah seedoh ah prohpohseetoh; ah seedoh seen kehrehr*
That's all right _____	No importa *noh eempohrtah*
Never mind _____	Déjelo *dehhehloh*
It could've happened to ___ anyone	Le puede pasar a cualquiera *leh pwehdeh pahsahr ah kwahlkyehrah*

Which do you prefer?_____	¿Qué prefiere?
	keh prehfyehreh?
What do you think?_____	¿Qué te parece?
	keh teh pahrehtheh?
Don't you like dancing? ____	¿No te gusta bailar?
	noh teh goostah bahylahr?
I don't mind_____	Me da igual
	meh dah eegwahl
Well done!_____	¡Muy bien!
	mwee byehn!
Not bad!_____	¡No está mal!
	noh ehstah mahl!
Great! _____	¡Excelente!
	ehxthehlehnteh!
Wonderful! _____	¡Qué delicia!
	keh dehleethyah!
It's really nice here! _____	¡Qué bien se está aquí!
	keh byehn seh ehstah ahkee!
How nice! _____	¡Qué mono/bonito!
	keh mohnoh/bohneetoh!
How nice for you! _____	¡Cuánto me alegro por usted!
	kwahntoh meh ahlehgroh pohr oostehdh!
I'm (not) very happy_____ with...	(No) estoy muy contento con...
	(noh) ehstoy mwee kohntehntoh kohn...
I'm glad..._____	Me alegro de que...
	meh ahlehgroh deh keh...
I'm having a great time ____	Me lo estoy pasando muy bien
	meh loh ehstoy pahsahndoh mwee byehn
I'm looking forward to it ___	Me hace ilusión
	meh ahtheh eeloosyohn
I hope it'll work out_____	Espero que salga bien
	ehspehroh keh sahlgah byehn
That's ridiculous!_____	¡Qué ridículo!
	keh reedeekooloh!
That's terrible! _____	¡Qué horrible!
	keh ohrreebleh!
What a pity! _____	¡Qué lástima!
	keh lahsteemah!
That's filthy! _____	¡Qué asco!
	keh ahskoh!
What a load of rubbish! ___	¡Qué tontería!
	keh tohntehreeah!
I don't like..._____	No me gusta...
	noh meh goostah...
I'm bored to death _____	Me aburro como una ostra
	meh ahboorroh kohmoh oonah ohstrah
I've had enough_____	Estoy harto(a)
	ehstoy ahrtoh(ah)
This is no good _____	No puede ser
	noh pwehdeh sehr
I was expecting _____ something completely different	Yo me había esperado otra cosa
	yoh meh ahbeeah ehspehrahdoh ohtrah kohsah

Conversation

3 Conversation

3.1 I beg your pardon?

I don't speak any/ I speak a little...	No hablo/hablo un poco de... *noh ahbloh/ahbloh oon pohkoh deh...*
I'm English	Soy inglés/inglesa *soy eenglehs/eenglehsah*
I'm Scottish	Soy escocés/escocesa *soy ehskohthehs/ehskothehsah*
I'm Irish	Soy irlandés/irlandesa *soy eerlahndehs/eerlahndehsah*
I'm Welsh	soy galés/galesa *soy gahlehs/gahlehsah*
Do you speak English/French/German?	¿Habla inglés/francés/alemán? *ahblah eenglehs/frahnthehs/ahlehmahn?*
Is there anyone who speaks...?	¿Hay alguien que hable...? *ay ahlguyehn keh ahbleh...?*
I beg your pardon?	¿Cómo dice? *kohmoh deetheh?*
I (don't) understand	(No) comprendo *(noh) kohmprehndoh*
Do you understand me?	¿Me entiende? *meh ehntyehndeh?*
Could you repeat that, please?	¿Le importa repetirlo? *leh eempohrtah rehpehteerloh?*
Could you speak more slowly, please?	¿Podría hablar más despacio? *pohdreeah ahblahr mahs dehspahthyo?*
What does that (word) mean?	¿Qué significa esto/esta palabra? *keh seegneefeekah ehstoh/ehstah pahlahbrah?*
Is that similar to/the same as...?	¿Es (más o menos) lo mismo que...? *ehs mahs oh mehnohs loh meesmoh keh...?*
Could you write that down for me, please?	¿Podría escribírmelo? *pohdreeah eskreebeermehloh?*
Could you spell that for me, please? *(See 1.8 Telephone alphabet)*	¿Podría deletreármelo? *pohdreeah dehlehtrehahrmehloh?*
Could you point that out in this phrase book, please?	¿Me lo podría señalar en esta guía? *meh loh pohdreeah sehnyahlahr ehn ehstah gheeah?*
One moment, please, I have to look it up	Espere que lo busco en la guía *ehspehreh keh loh booskoh ehn lah gheeah*
I can't find the word/the sentence	No puedo encontrar la palabra/la frase *noh pwehdoh ehnkohntrahr lah pahlahbrah/lah frahseh*
How do you say that in...?	¿Cómo se dice eso en...? *kohmoh seh deetheh ehstoh ehn...?*
How do you pronounce that?	¿Cómo se pronuncia? *kohmoh seh prohnoonthyah?*

25

May I introduce myself?	Permítame presentarme *pehrmeetahmeh prehsehntahrmeh*
My name's...	Me llamo... *meh lyahmoh...*
I'm...	Soy... *soy...*
What's your name?	¿Cómo se llama? *kohmoh seh lyahmah?*
May I introduce...?	Permítame presentarle a... *pehrmeetahmeh prehsehntahrleh ah...*
This is my wife/ daughter/mother/ girlfriend	Esta es mi mujer/mi hija/mi madre/mi amiga *ehstah ehs mee moohehr/mee eehah /mee mahdreh/mee ahmeegah*
– my husband/son/ father/boyfriend.	Este es mi marido/mi hijo/mi padre/mi amigo *ehsteh ehs mee mahreedoh/mee eehoh/mee pahdreh/mee ahmeegoh*
How do you do	Hola, mucho gusto *ohlah, moochoh goostoh*
Pleased to meet you	Encantado(a) (de conocerle) *ehnkahntahdoh(ah) (deh kohnohthehrleh)*
Where are you from?	¿De dónde es usted? *deh dohndeh ehs oostehdh?*
I'm from England/Scotland/ Ireland/Wales	Soy inglés/esa escocés/esa irlandés/esa galés/esa *soy eenglehs/ehsah ehskohthehs/ehsah eerlahndehs/ehsah gahlehs/ ehsah*
What city do you live in?	¿En qué ciudad vive? *ehn keh thyoodahdh beebeh?*
In..., It's near...	En...Eso está cerca de... *ehn...ehsoh ehstah thehrkah deh...*
Have you been here long?	¿Hace mucho que está aquí? *ahtheh moochoh keh ehstah ahkee?*
A few days	Unos días *oonohs deeahs*
How long are you staying here?	¿Cuánto tiempo piensa quedarse? *kwahntoh tyehmpoh pyehnsah kehdahrseh?*
We're (probably) leaving tomorrow/ in two weeks	Nos iremos (probablemente) mañana/dentro de dos semanas *nohs eerehmohs (prohbahblehmehnteh) mahnyahnah/dehntroh deh dohs sehmahnahs*
Where are you staying?	¿Dónde se aloja? *dohndeh seh ahlohhah?*
In a hotel/an apartment	En un hotel/apartamento *ehn oon ohtehl/ahpahrtahmehntoh*
On a camp site	En un camping *ehn oon kahmpeen*
With friends/relatives	En casa de amigos/parientes *ehn kahsah deh ahmeegohs/pahryehntehs*
Are you here on your own/with your family?	¿Ha venido solo(a)/con su familia? *ah behneedoh sohloh(ah)/kohn soo fahmeelyah?*

I'm on my own _____	He venido solo(a)
	eh behneedoh sohloh(ah)
I'm with my _____	con mi pareja/mujer/marido
partner/wife/husband	*kohn mee pahrehhah/moohehr/mahreedoh*
– with my family _____	con mi familia
	kohn mee fahmeelyah
– with relatives _____	con unos parientes
	kohn oonohs pahryehntehs
– with a friend/friends _____	con un amigo/una amiga/unos amigos
	kohn oon ahmeegoh/oonah
	ahmeegah/oonohs ahmeegohs
Are you married? _____	¿Está casado/casada?
	ehstah kahsahdoh/kahsahdah?
Do you have a steady _____	¿Tienes novio/novia?
boyfriend/girlfriend?	*tyehnehs nohbyoh/nohbyah?*
That's none of your _____	No es asunto suyo
business.	*noh ehs ahsoontoh sooyoh*
I'm married _____	Soy casado
	soy kahsahdoh
– single _____	Soy soltero
	soy sohltehroh
– separated _____	Estoy separado
	ehstoy sehpahrahdoh
– divorced _____	Estoy divorciado
	ehstoy deebohrthyahdoh
– a widow/widower _____	Soy viuda/viudo
	soy byoodah/byoodoh
I live alone/with _____	Vivo solo(a)/con otra persona
someone	*beeboh sohloh(ah)/kohn ohtrah*
	pehrsohnah
Do you have any _____	¿Tiene hijos/nietos?
children/grandchildren?	*tyehneh eehohs/nyehtohs?*
How old are you? _____	¿Cuántos años tiene?
	kwahntohs ahnyohs tyehneh?
How old is she/he? _____	¿Cuántos años tiene?
	kwahntohs ahnyohs tyehneh?
I'm... _____	Tengo...años
	tehngoh...ahnyohs
She's/he's... _____	Tiene...años
	tyehneh...ahnyohs
What do you do for a _____	¿En qué trabaja?
living?	*ehn keh trahbahhah?*
I work in an office _____	Trabajo en una oficina
	trahbahhoh ehn oonah ohfeetheenah
I'm a student/ _____	Estudio
I'm at school	*ehstoodyoh*
I'm unemployed _____	Estoy en paro
	ehstoy ehn pahroh
I'm retired _____	Soy jubilado
	soy hoobeelahdoh
I'm on a disability _____	Tengo una pensión de invalidez
pension	*tehngoh oonah pehnsyohn deh*
	eenbahleedeth
I'm a housewife _____	Soy ama de casa
	soy ahmah deh kahsah
Do you like your job? _____	¿Le gusta su trabajo?
	leh goostah soo trahbahhoh?

Most of the time _____	A veces sí, a veces no
	ah behthehs see, ah behthehs noh
I usually do, but I prefer ___ holidays	Por lo general sí, pero prefiero las vacaciones
	pohr loh hehnehrahl see, pehroh prehfyehroh lahs bahkahthyohnehs

3.3 Starting/ending a conversation

Could I ask you _____ something?	¿Podría preguntarle una cosa?
	pohdreeah prehgoontahrleh oonah kohsah?
Excuse me	Perdone
	pehrdohneh
Excuse me, could you _____ help me?	¿Podría ayudarme?
	pohdreeah ahyoodahrmeh?
Yes, what's the problem? __	Sí, ¿qué pasa?
	see, keh pahsah?
What can I do for you? ____	¿En qué puedo servirle?
	ehn keh pwehdoh sehrbeerleh?
Sorry, I don't have time now	Lo siento, ahora no tengo tiempo
	loh syehntoh, ahohrah noh tehngoh tyehmpoh
Do you have a light? _____	¿Tiene fuego?
	tyehneh fwehgoh?
May I join you? _____	¿Le importa que me siente?
	leh eempohrtah keh meh syehnteh?
Could you take a _____ picture of me/us? Press this button.	¿Podría sacarme/sacarnos una foto? Hay que apretar este botón
	pohdreeah sahkahrmeh/sahkahrnohs oonah fohtoh? ay keh ahprehtahr ehsteh bohtohn
Leave me alone _____	Déjeme en paz
	dehhehmeh ehn pahth
Get lost_____	Váyase al diablo
	bahyahseh ahl deeahbloh
Go away or I'll scream_____	Como no se vaya, grito
	kohmoh noh seh bahyah, greetoh

3.4 Congratulations and condolences

Happy birthday/many happy returns	Feliz cumpleaños/felicidades
	fehleeth koomplehahnyohs/fehleetheedahdehs
Please accept my condolences.	Le acompaño en el sentimiento
	leh ahkohmpahnyoh ehn ehl sehnteemyehntoh
I'm very sorry for you _____	¡Cuánto lo siento por usted!
	kwahntoh loh syehntoh pohr oostehdh!

3.5 A chat about the weather

See also 1.5 The weather

It's so hot/cold today!_____	¡Qué calor/frío hace hoy!
	keh kahlohr/freeoh ahtheh oy!
Nice weather, isn't it?_____	¡Qué buen tiempo hace! ¿Verdad?
	keh bwehn tyehmpoh ahtheh! behrdah?

What a wind/storm! _____	¡Vaya viento/tormenta!
	bahyah byehntoh/tohrmentah!
All that rain/snow! _____	¡Cómo llueve/nieva!
	kohmoh lywehbeh/nyehbah!
All that fog! _____	¡Cuánta niebla!
	kwahntah nyehblah!
Has the weather been _____ like this for long here?	¿Hace mucho que hace este tiempo?
	ahtheh moochoh keh ahtheh ehsteh tyehmpoh?
Is it always this hot/cold ___ here?	¿Aquí siempre hace tanto calor/frío?
	ahkee syehmpreh ahtheh tahntoh kahlohr/freeoh?
Is it always this dry/wet____ here?	¿Aquí siempre hace un tiempo tan seco/lluvioso?
	ahkee syehmpreh ahtheh oon tyehmpoh tahn sehkoh/lyoobyohsoh?

.6 Hobbies

Do you have any _____ hobbies?	¿Tiene algún hobby?
	tyehnneh algoon <u>h</u>ohbee?
I like painting/_____ reading/photography/ DIY	Me gusta pintar/leer/la fotografía/el bricolaje
	meh goostah peentahr/lehehr/lah fohtohgrahfeeah/ehl breekohlah<u>h</u>eh
I like music _____	Me gusta la música
	meh goostah lah mooseekah
I like playing the _____ guitar/piano	Me gusta tocar la guitarra/el piano
	meh goostah tohkahr lah gueetahrrah/ehl pyahnoh
I like going to the movies __	Me gusta ir al cine
	meh goostah eer ahl theeneh
I like travelling/_____ sport/fishing/walking	Me gusta viajar/hacer deporte/pescar/salir a caminar
	meh goostah byah<u>h</u>ahr/ahthehr dehpohrteh/pehskahr/sahleer ah kahmeenahr

.7 Being the host(ess)

See also 4 Eating out

Can I offer you a drink? ____	¿Le gustaría algo de beber?
	leh goostahreeah ahlgoh deh behbehr?
What would you like_____ to drink?	¿Qué quieres beber?
	keh kyehrehs behbehr?
Something non-alcoholic,___ please.	Algo sin alcohol
	ahlgoh seen ahlkohl
Would you like a _____ cigarette/cigar/to roll your own?	¿Quiere un cigarrillo/un puro/liar un cigarrillo?
	kyehreh oon theegahrreelyoh/oon pooroh/leeahr oon theegahrreelyoh?
I don't smoke _____	No fumo
	noh foomoh

3.8 Invitations

Conversation

Are you doing anything tonight?	¿Tiene algo que hacer esta noche?
	tyehneh ahlgoh keh ahthehr ehstah nohcheh?
Do you have any plans for today/this afternoon/tonight?	¿Ya tiene planes para hoy/esta tarde/esta noche?
	yah tyehneh plahnehs pahrah oy/ehstah tahrdeh/ehstah nohcheh?
Would you like to go out with me?	¿Le(te) apetece salir conmigo?
	leh(teh) ahpehtehtheh sahleer kohnmeegoh?
Would you like to go dancing with me?	¿Le(te) apetece ir a bailar conmigo?
	leh(teh) ahpehtehtheh eer ah baylahr kohnmeegoh?
Would you like to have lunch/dinner with me?	¿Le(te) apetece comer/cenar conmigo?
	leh(teh) ahpehtehtheh kohmehr/thenahr kohnmeegoh?
Would you like to come to the beach with me?	¿Le(te) apetece ir a la playa conmigo?
	leh(teh) ahpehtehtheh eer ah lah plahyah kohnmeegoh?
Would you like to come into town with us?	¿Le apetece ir a la ciudad con nosotros?
	leh ahpehtehtheh eer ah lah thyoodahdh kohn nohsohtrohs?
Would you like to come and see some friends with us?	¿Le apetece ir a casa de unos amigos con nosotros?
	leh ahpehtehtheh eer ah kahsah deh oonohs ahmeegohs kohn nohsohtrohs?
Shall we dance?	¿Bailamos?
	baylahmohs?
– sit at the bar?	¿Vienes a sentarte conmigo en la barra?
	byehnehs ah sehntahrteh kohnmeegoh ehn lah bahrrah?
– get something to drink?	¿Vamos a beber algo?
	bahmohs ah behbehr ahlgoh?
– go for a walk/drive?	¿Vamos a dar una vuelta?
	bahmohs ah dahr oonah bwehltah?
Yes, all right	Sí, vamos
	see, bahmohs
Good idea	Buena idea
	bwehnah eedehah
No (thank you)	No (gracias)
	noh (grahthyahs)
Maybe later	Quizá más tarde
	keethah mahs tahrdeh
I don't feel like it	No me apetece
	noh meh ahpehtehtheh
I don't have time	No tengo tiempo
	noh tehngoh tyehmpoh
I already have a date	Ya tengo otro compromiso
	yah tehngoh ohtroh kohmprohmeesoh
I'm not very good at dancing/volleyball/swimming	No sé bailar/jugar al vóleibol/nadar
	noh seh baylahr/<u>h</u>oogahr ahl vohleheebohl/nahdahr

3 .9 Paying a compliment

You look wonderful! _____ ¡Qué guapo/guapa está(estás)!
keh wahpoh/wahpah ehstah(ehstahs)!

I like your car! _____ ¡Qué bonito coche!
keh bohneetoh kohcheh!

I like your ski outfit! _____ ¡Qué bonito traje de esquiar!
keh bohneetoh trahheh deh ehskeeahr!

You're a nice boy/girl _____ Eres muy bueno/buena
ehrehs mwee bwehnoh/bwehnah

What a sweet child! _____ ¡Qué niño tan majo/niña tan maja!
keh neenyoh tahn mahhoh/neenyah tahn mahhah!

You're a wonderful _____ Bailas muy bien
dancer! *bahylahs mwee byehn*

You're a wonderful _____ Cocinas muy bien
cook! *kohtheenahs mwee byehn*

You're a terrific soccer _____ Juegas muy bien al fútbol
player! *hwehgahs mwee byehn ahl footbohl*

3 .10 Chatting someone up

I like being with you _____ Me gusta estar contigo
meh goostah ehstahr kohnteegoh

I've missed you so much ___ Te he echado mucho de menos
teh eh ehchahdoh moochoh deh mehnohs

I dreamt about you _____ He soñado contigo
eh sohnyahdoh kohnteegoh

I think about you all day ___ Pienso todo el día en ti
pyehnsoh tohdoh ehl deeah ehn tee

You have such a sweet _____ Tienes una sonrisa muy bonita
smile *tyehnehs oonah sohnreesah mwee bohneetah*

You have such beautiful ___ Tienes unos ojos muy bonitos
eyes *tyehnehs oonohs ohhohs mwee bohneetohs*

I'm in love with you _____ Estoy enamorado/enamorada de ti
ehstoy ehnahmohrahdoh/ehnahmohrahdah deh tee

I'm in love with you too ___ Yo también de ti
yoh tahmbyehn deh tee

I love you _____ Te quiero
teh kyehroh

I love you too _____ Yo también a ti
yoh tahmbyehn ah tee

I don't feel as strongly _____ Yo no siento lo mismo por ti
about you *yoh noh syehntoh loh meesmoh pohr tee*

I already have a _____ Ya tengo pareja
boyfriend/girlfriend *yah tehngoh pahrehhah*

I'm not ready for that_____ Yo no estoy preparado(a)
yoh noh ehstoy prehpahrahdoh/ah

This is going too fast _____ Vamos demasiado rápido
for me *bahmohs dehmahsyahdoh rahpeedoh*

Take your hands off me___ No me toque(s)
noh meh tohkeh(s)

Okay, no problem _____ Vale, no importa
bahleh, noh eempohrtah

Will you stay with me tonight?	¿Te quedas a dormir?
	teh kehdahs ah dohrmeer?
I'd like to go to bed with you	Me gustaría acostarme contigo
	meh goostahreeah ahkohstahrmeh kohnteegoh
Only if we use a condom	Sólo si usamos condón
	sohloh see oosahmohs kohndohn
We have to be careful about AIDS	Hay que tener cuidado por lo del Sida
	ay keh tehnehr kweedahdoh pohr loh dehl seedah
That's what they all say	Eso es lo que dicen todos
	ehsoh ehs loh keh deethehn tohdohs
We shouldn't take any risks	Más vale no arriesgarse
	mahs bahleh noh ahrryehsgahrseh
Do you have a condom?	¿Llevas condones?
	lyehbahs kohndohnehs?
No? In that case we won't do it	¿No? Pues entonces no
	noh? pwehs ehntohnthehs noh

3 .11 Arrangements

When will I see you again?	¿Cuándo te veo?
	kwahndoh the behoh?
Are you free over the weekend?	¿Tiene tiempo este fin de semana?
	tyehneh tyehmpoh ehsteh feen deh sehmahnah?
What shall we arrange?	¿Cómo quedamos?
	kohmoh kehdahmohs?
Where shall we meet?	¿Dónde nos encontramos?
	dohndeh nohs ehnkohntrahmohs?
Will you pick me/us up?	¿Me/nos pasa a buscar?
	meh/nohs pahsah ah booskahr?
Shall I pick you up?	¿Lo/la paso a buscar?
	loh/lah pahsoh ah booskahr?
I have to be home by...	Tengo que estar en casa a las...
	tehngoh keh ehstahr ehn kahsah ah lahs...
I don't want to see you anymore	No quiero volver a verlo/verla
	noh kyehroh bohlbehr ah behrloh/behrlah

3 .12 Saying goodbye

Can I take you home?	¿Lo/la acompaño a su casa?
	loh/lah ahkohmpahnyoh ah soo kahsah?
Can I write/call you?	¿Puedo escribirle/llamarlo/llamarla por teléfono?
	pwehdoh ehskreebeerleh /lyahmahrloh/ lyahmahrlah pohr tehlehfohnoh?
Will you write/call me?	¿Me escribirá/llamará por teléfono?
	meh ehskreebeerah/lyahmahrah pohr tehlehfohnoh?
Can I have your address/phone number?	¿Me da su dirección/número de teléfono?
	meh dah soo deerehkthyohn/noomehroh deh tehlehfohnoh?
Thanks for everything	Gracias por todo
	grahthyahs pohr tohdoh
It was very nice	Lo hemos pasado muy bien
	loh ehmohs pahsahdoh mwee byehn

Say hello to...	Recuerdos a...
	rehkwehrdohs ah...
All the best	Te deseo lo mejor
	teh dehsehoh loh meh<u>h</u>ohr
Good luck	Que te vaya bien
	keh teh bahyah byehn
When will you be back?	¿Cuándo vuelves?
	kwahndoh bwehlbehs?
I'll be waiting for you	Te esperaré
	the ehspehrahreh.
I'd like to see you again	Me gustaría volver a verte
	meh goostahreeah bohlbehr ah behrteh
I hope we meet again soon	Espero que nos volvamos a ver pronto
	ehspehroh keh nohs bohlbahmohs ah behr prohntoh
This is our address. If you're ever in the UK	Esta es nuestra dirección. Si alguna vez pasa por el Reino Unido...
	ehstah ehs nwehstrah deerehkthyohn. see ahlgoonah behth pahsah pohr ehl reheenoh ooneedoh...
You'd be more than welcome	Está cordialmente invitado
	ehstah kohrdyahlmehnteh eenbeetahdoh

3

Conversation

Eating out

4 **E**ating out

● **In Spain** people usually have three meals:
1 *El desayuno* (breakfast) approximately between 7 and 10 am.
Breakfast is light and consists of *café con leche* (white coffee), a
croissant or *suizo* (light sugary bun) or *tostadas* (toast).
2 *El almuerzo* (lunch) approx. between 2 and 4 pm, though hotels
usually serve at standard times. Lunch always includes a hot dish and
is the most important meal of the day. Office workers and
schoolchildren still lunch at home. It usually consists of four courses:
– starter (which can be a plate of greens)
– main course
– dessert
– fruit
3 *La cena* (dinner) between 9 and 11pm, 8pm in most hotels. Dinner is
usually a light, hot meal, taken with the family.
At around 6 or 7pm, a snack (*la merienda*) is often served, consisting
frequently of sandwiches with *chorizo* or *jamón serrano* and *pastas*
(biscuits) or small cakes.
Pinchos and *tapas* are often taken at bars with an apéritif, either in the
late morning or the evening.

4 .1 **O**n arrival

I'd like to book a table for seven o'clock, please	¿Podría reservar una mesa para las siete? *pohdreeah rehsehrbahr oonah mehsah pahrah lahs syehteh?*
I'd like a table for two, please	Quisiera una mesa para dos personas *keesyehrah oonah mehsah pahrah dohs pehrsohnahs*
We've/we haven't booked	(No) hemos reservado *(noh) ehmohs rehsehrbahdoh*
Is the restaurant open yet?	¿Ya está abierto el restaurante? *yah ehstah ahbyehrtoh ehl rehstahoorahnteh?*
What time does the restaurant open/close?	¿A qué hora abre/cierra el restaurante? *ah keh ohrah ahbreh/thyehrah ehl rehstahoorahnteh?*
Can we wait for a table?	¿Podemos esperar hasta que se desocupe una mesa? *pohdehmohs ehspehrahr ahstah keh seh dehsohkoopeh oonah mehsah?*
Do we have to wait long?	¿Tenemos que esperar mucho? *tehnehmohs keh ehspehrahr moochoh?*

¿Ha reservado mesa?	Do you have a reservation?
¿A nombre de quién?	What name, please?
Por aquí, por favor.	This way, please
Esta mesa está reservada	This table is reserved
En quince minutos quedará libre una mesa	We'll have a table free in fifteen minutes.
¿Le importaría esperar (en la barra)	Would you like to wait (at the bar)?

Is this seat taken? _____	¿Está ocupada esta silla?
	ehstah ohkoopahdah ehstah seelyah?
Could we sit here/there? ___	¿Podemos sentarnos aquí/allí?
	pohdemohs sehntahrnohs ahkee/ahlyee?
Can we sit by the_____ window?	¿Podemos sentarnos junto a la ventana?
	pohdehmohs sehntahrnohs hoontoh ah lah behntahnah?
Can we eat outside? _____	¿Podemos comer afuera?
	pohdehmohs kohmehr ahfwehrah?
Do you have another _____ chair for us?	¿Podría traernos otra silla?
	pohdreeah trahehrnohs ohtrah seelyah?
Do you have a _____ highchair?	¿Podría traernos una silla para niños?
	pohdreeah trahehrnohs oonah seelyah pahrah neenyohs?
Is there a socket for _____ this bottle-warmer?	¿Hay un enchufe para este calentador de biberones?
	ay oon ehnchoofeh pahrah ehsteh kahlehntahdohr deh beebehrohnehs?
Could you warm up _____ this bottle/jar for me?	¿Podría calentarme este biberón/este bote?
	pohdreeah kahlehntahrmeh ehsteh beebehrohn/ehsteh bohteh?
Not too hot, please _____	Que no esté muy caliente, por favor
	keh noh ehsteh mwee kahlyehnteh pohr fahbohr
Is there somewhere I _____ can change the baby's nappy?	¿Hay algún lugar para cambiar al bebé?
	ay ahlgoon loogahr pahrah kahmbyahr ahl behbeh?
Where are the toilets? _____	¿Dónde están los servicios?
	dohnde ehstahn lohs sehrbeethyohs?

4 .2 Ordering

Waiter! _____	¡Camarero!
	kahmahrehroh!
Madam!/Sir! _____	¡Oiga, (por favor)!
	oygah (pohr fahbohr)!
We'd like something to ____ eat/a drink	Quisiéramos comer/beber algo
	keesyehrahmohs kohmehr/behber ahlgoh
Could I have a quick_____ meal?	¿Podría comer algo rápido?
	pohdreeah kohmehr ahlgoh rahpeedoh?
We don't have much _____ time	Tenemos poco tiempo
	tehnehmohs pohkoh tyehmpoh
We'd like to have a _____ drink first	Antes quisiéramos beber algo
	ahntehs keesyehrahmohs behbehr ahlgoh
Could we see the_____ menu/wine list, please?	¿Nos podría traer la carta/la carta de vinos?
	nohs pohdreeah trahehr lah kahrtah/lah kahrtah deh beenohs?
Do you have a menu _____ in English?	¿Tienen menú en inglés?
	tyehnehn mehnoo ehn eenglehs?
Do you have a dish_____ of the day?	¿Tienen menú del día/menú turístico?
	tyehnehn mehnoo dehl deeah/mehnoo tooreesteekoh?
We haven't made a _____ choice yet	Todavía no hemos elegido
	tohdahbeeah noh ehmohs ehleheedoh

What do you recommend?	¿Qué nos recomienda?
	keh nohs rehkohmyehndah?
What are the specialities of the region/the house?	¿Cuáles son las especialidades de la región/de la casa?
	kwahlehs sohn lahs ehspehthyahleedahdehs deh lah rehhyohn/deh lah kahsah?
I like strawberries/olives	Me gustan las fresas/las aceitunas
	meh goostahn lahs frehsahs/lahs ahtheheetoonahs
I don't like meat/fish/...	No me gusta el pescado/la carne/...
	noh meh goostah ehl pehskahdoh/lah kahrneh/...
What's this?	¿Qué es esto?
	keh ehs ehstoh?
Does it have...in it?	¿Lleva...?
	lyehbah...?
What does it taste like?	¿A qué sabe?
	ah keh sahbeh?
Is this a hot or a cold dish?	¿Es un plato caliente o frío?
	ehs oon plahtoh kahlyehnyteh oh freeoh?
Is this sweet?	¿Es un plato dulce?
	ehs oon plahtoh doolthe?
Is this spicy?	¿Es un plato picante?
	ehs oon plahtoh peekahnteh?
Do you have anything else, please?	¿Tendría otra cosa?
	tehndreeah ohtrah kohsah?
I'm on a salt-free diet	No puedo comer sal
	noh pwehdoh kohmehr sahl
I can't eat pork	No puedo comer carne de cerdo
	noh pwehdoh kohmehr kahrneh deh thehrdoh
– sugar	No puedo comer azúcar
	noh pwehdo kohmehr ahthookahr
– fatty foods	No puedo comer grasa
	noh pwehdoh kohmehr grahsah
– (hot) spices	No puedo comer cosas picantes
	noh pwehdoh kohmehr kohsahs peekahntehs
I'll/we'll have what those people are having	Lo mismo que esos señores, por favor
	loh meesmoh keh ehsohs sehnyohrehs pohr fahbohr

4 Eating out

¿Van a tomar un aperitivo?	Would you like a drink first?
¿Ya han elegido?	Have you decided?
¿Qué van a tomar?	What would you like to eat?
Que aproveche	Enjoy your meal.
¿Quiere su bistec rojo, mediano o muy hecho?	Would you like your steak rare, medium or well done?
¿Van a tomar postre/café?	Would you like a dessert/coffee?

37

English	Spanish
I'd like... _____	Para mí... *pahrah mee...*
We're not having a _____ starter	No vamos a comer primer plato *noh bahmohs ah kohmehr preemehr plahtoh*
The child will share_____ what we're having	El niño/la niña comerá de nuestro menú *ehl neenyoh/lah neenyah kohmehrah deh nwehstroh mehnoo*
Could I have some _____ more bread, please?	Más pan, por favor *mahs pahn pohr fahbohr*
– a bottle of water/wine____	Otra botella de agua/de vino, por favor *ohtrah bohtehlyah deh ahgwah/deh beenoh, pohr fahbohr*
– another helping of... ____	Otra ración de..., por favor *ohtrah rahthyohn deh..., pohr fahbohr*
– some salt and pepper____	¿Podría traerme sal y pimienta? *pohdreeah trahehrmeh sahl ee peemyehntah?*
– a napkin _____	¿Podría traerme una servilleta? *pohdreeah trahehrmeh oonah sehrbeelyehtah?*
– a spoon_____	¿Podría traerme una cuchara? *pohdreeah trahehrmeh oonah koochahrah?*
– an ashtray _____	¿Podría traerme un cenicero? *pohdreeah trahehrmeh oon thehneethehroh?*
– some matches_____	¿Podría traerme unas cerillas? *pohdreeah trahehrmeh oonahs thehreelyahs?*
– some toothpicks _____	¿Podría traerme unos palillos? *pohdreeah trahehrmeh oonohs pahleelyohs?*
– a glass of water _____	¿Podría traerme un vaso de agua? *pohdreeah trahehrmeh oon bahsoh deh ahgwah?*
– a straw (for the child) ___	¿Podría traerme una pajita (para el niño/ la niña)? *pohdreeah trahehrmeh oonah pahheetah (pahrah ehl neenyoh/lah neenyah)?*
Enjoy your meal!_____	¡Que aproveche! *keh ahprohbehcheh!*
You too! _____	Igualmente *eegwahlmehnteh*
Cheers!_____	¡Salud! *sahloodh!*
The next round's on me ___	La próxima ronda la pago yo *lah prohxeemah rohndah lah pahgoh yoh*
Could we have a doggy____ bag, please?	¿Podemos llevarnos las sobras? *pohdehmohs lyehbarnohs lahs sohbrahs?*

4.3 The bill

See also 8.2 Settling the bill

English	Spanish
How much is this dish? ____	¿Cuánto vale este plato? *kwahntoh bahleh ehsteh plahtoh?*
Could I have the bill, _____ please?	La cuenta, por favor *lah kwehntah, pohr fahbohr*
All together _____	Todo junto *tohdoh hoontoh*

Everyone pays separately	Cada uno paga lo suyo
	kahdah oonoh pahgah loh sooyoh
Could we have the menu again, please?	¿Podría traernos otra vez la carta?
	pohdreeah trahehrnohs ohtrah behth lah kahrtah?
The...is not on the bill	Ha olvidado apuntar el/la...
	ah olbeedahdoh ahpoontahr ehl/lah...

4 .4 Complaints

It's taking a very long time	Están tardando mucho
	ehstahn tahrdahndoh moochoh
We've been here an hour already	Ya llevamos una hora aquí
	yah lyebahmohs oonah ohrah ahkee
This must be a mistake	Esto tiene que ser una equivocación
	ehstoh tyehneh keh sehr oonah ehkeebohkahthyohn
This is not what I ordered	Esto no es lo que he pedido
	ehstoh noh ehs loh keh eh pehdeedoh
I ordered...	He pedido...
	eh pehdeedoh
There's a dish missing	Falta un plato
	fahltah oon plahtoh
This is broken/not clean	Esto está roto/no está limpio
	ehstoh ehstah rohtoh/noh ehstah leempyoh
The food's cold	La comida está fría
	lah kohmeedah ehstah freeah
– not fresh	La comida no es fresca
	lah kohmeedah noh ehs frehskah
– too salty/sweet/spicy	La comida está muy salada/dulce/picante
	lah kohmeedah ehstah mwee sahlahdah/doolteh/peekahnteh
The meat's not done	La carne está cruda
	lah kahrneh ehstah kroodah
– overdone	La carne está muy hecha
	lah kahrneh ehstah mwee ehchah
– tough	La carne está dura
	lah kahrneh ehstah doorah
– off	La carne está podrida
	lah kahrneh ehstah pohdreedah
Could I have something else instead of this?	¿Me podría traer otra cosa en lugar de esto?
	meh pohdreeah trahehr ohtrah kohsah ehn loogahr deh ehstoh?
The bill/this amount is not right	La cuenta/este precio está mal
	lah kwehntah/ehsteh prehthyoh ehstah mahl
We didn't have this	Esto no lo hemos comido/bebido
	ehstoh noh loh ehmohs kohmeedoh/behbeedoh
There's no paper in the toilet	No hay papel en el servicio
	noh ay pahpehl ehn ehl sehrbeethyoh
Do you have a complaints book?	¿Tienen libro de quejas?
	tyehnen leebroh deh keh<u>h</u>as?
Will you call the manager, please?	Haga el favor de llamar al jefe
	ahgah ehl fahbohr deh lyamahr ahl <u>h</u>ehfeh

That was a wonderful _____ meal	Hemos comido muy bien
	ehmohs kohmeedoh mwee byehn
The food was excellent _____	La comida ha estado exquisita
	lah kohmeedah ah ehstahdoh ehxkeeseetah
The...in particular was _____ delicious	Sobre todo nos ha gustado el/la...
	sohbreh tohdoh nohs ah goostahdoh ehl/lah...

4 .6 The menu

aperitivo	mariscos	postres
apéritif	**seafood**	**sweets/dessert**
aves	pastelería	primeros platos
poultry	**pastry**	**starters**
azúcar	pescados	raciones
sugar	**fish**	**portions**
bebidas alcohólicas	platos calientes	servicio incluido
alcoholic beverages	**hot dishes**	**service included**
bebidas calientes	platos combinados	sopas
hot beverages	**combined dishes**	**soups**
carta de vinos	plato del día	tapas
wine list	**dish of the day**	**tapas**
cócteles	platos fríos	venado
cocktails	**cold dishes**	**game**
cubierto	platos principales	verduras
cover charge	**main courses**	**vegetables**
entremeses variados	platos típicos	
hors d'oeuvres	**regional specialities**	

4 .7 Alphabetical list of drinks and dishes

aceituna	anís	biftec
olive	**aniseed**	**steak**
aguacate	apio	bizcocho (borracho)
avocado	**celery**	**sponge cake(with**
ajo	arenque	**sherry or similar)**
garlic	**herring**	bocadillo
albóndigas	arroz	**sandwich**
meat balls	**rice**	buey/vaca
alcachofa	asado	**beef**
artichoke	**roast, roasted**	cabrito
almejas	atún/bonito	**kid**
clams	**tuna**	café (solo/con leche)
almendras	avellana	**coffee (black/white)**
almonds	**hazelnut**	calamares (en su
ancas de rana	bacalao	**tinta)**
frog's legs	**cod**	**squid (cooked in**
anchoa/boquerón	batido de...	**their ink)**
anchovy	**...milk shake**	caldo
anguila	berenjena	**broth**
eel	**aubergine**	callos
		tripe

Spanish	English
cangrejo	crab
caracoles	snails
carne	meat
carpa	carp
castaña	chestnut
cebolla	onion
cerdo	pork
cerezas	cherries
cerveza	beer
chorizo	chorizo (paprika flavoured salami sausage)
chucrut	sauerkraut
chuleta/costilla	chop
churros	fritters
ciervo	venison
cigalas	Dublin Bay prawns
ciruela	plum
cochinillo asado	roast suckling pig
cocido	boiled
codorniz	quail
col/berza	cabbage
coles de Bruselas	Brussels sprouts
coliflor	cauliflower
coñac	brandy
conejo	rabbit
copa helada/helado	ice cream
cordero	lamb
crema/nata	cream
criadillas/mollejas	sweetbreads
crudo	raw
cuba libre	rum coke
dátil	date
dulce	sweet
emperador	swordfish
en escabeche	pickled
endibia	chicory/endive
ensalada (mixta)	mixed salad
ensaladilla rusa	Russian salad
escalope	escalope
espárragos	asparagus
especies	spices
espinaca	spinach
fideos	noodles
filete	fillet
flan	cream caramel
frambuesa	raspberry
fresa	strawberry
frito	fried
fruta (del tiempo)	seasonal fruit
galleta	biscuit
gambas	prawns
garbanzos	chick peas
gazpacho andaluz	gazpacho (cold soup)
granizado de limón/café	iced drink (lemon/coffee)
grosellas	red/black currants
guisado	stew
guisantes	peas
habas	broad beans
harina	flour
hígado de oca	goose liver
higo	fig
huevos al plato/duros/revueltos	fried/hard boiled/scrambled eggs
jamón de York/serrano	ham (cooked/Parma style)
jerez (seco, dulce)	sherry (dry, sweet)
judías verdes	French beans
jugo/zumo	fruit juice
langosta	lobster
langostino	crayfish
leche	milk
lechuga	lettuce
legumbres	vegetables (legumes)
lengua	tongue
lenguado	sole
lentejas	lentils
licor	liqueur
liebre	hare
limón	lemon
lomo de cerdo	tenderloin of pork

maíz (mazorca)
corn (on the cob)
mantequilla
butter
manzana
apple
mazapán
marzipan
mejillones
mussels
melocotón (en
  almíbar)
peach (in syrup)
melón
melon
membrillo
quince
merluza
hake
mermelada
jam
mero
sea bass
morcilla
black pudding
mostaza
mustard
muslo de pollo
drumstick
nuez
walnut
ostras
oysters
paella
paella
pan
bread
pastel
cake
patatas fritas
chips/crisps
pato (silvestre)
(wild) duck
pechuga (de pollo)
(chicken) breast
pepino
cucumber
pepinillos
gherkins
pera
pear

perdiz
partridge
perejil
parsley
pescado
fish
picadillo de ternera
minced veal
pierna (de cordero)
leg (of lamb)
pimentón
paprika
pimienta
pepper
pimientos
green/red peppers
piña
pineapple
plancha (a la)
grilled
plátano
banana
plato principal
main course
platos típicos
regional specialities
pollo
chicken
puerro
leek
pulpo
octopus
queso
cheese
rábanos
radishes
rabo de buey
oxtail
rape
monkfish
remolacha
beetroot
riñones
kidneys
rodaballo
turbot
romana (a la)
deep fried
vino rosado
rosé wine
salchicha
sausage

salchichón
salami
salmón
salmon
salmón ahumado
smoked salmon
salmonete
red mullet
sandía
water melon
sangría
sangría
sardinas
sardines
setas
mushrooms
solomillo de buey
fillet of beef
sopa
soup
tarta helada
ice cream cake
ternera
veal
tinto
red wine
tocino
bacon
tortilla española
Spanish omelette
  (potato)
tortilla francesa
plain omelette
tortitas
waffles
trucha
trout
trufas
truffles
turrón
nougat
uvas
grapes
verduras
green vegetables
vinagre
vinegar
zanahorias
carrots
zumo de naranja
orange juice

On the road

5 On the road

5.1 Asking for directions

Excuse me, could I ask you something?	Perdone, ¿podría preguntarle algo?
	pehrdohneh, pohdreeah prehgoontahrleh ahlgoh?
I've lost my way	Me he perdido
	meh eh pehrdeedoh
Is there a(n)... around here?	¿Sabe dónde hay un(a)...por aquí?
	sahbeh dohndeh ay oon(ah)...pohr ahkee?
Is this the way to...?	¿Se va por aquí a...?
	seh bah pohr ahkee ah...?
Could you tell me how to get to the... (name of place) by car/on foot?	¿Podría decirme cómo llegar a... (en coche/a pie)?
	pohdreeah dehtheermeh kohmoh lyehgahr ah... (ehn kohcheh/ah pyeh)?
What's the quickest way to...?	¿Cómo hago para llegar lo antes posible a...?
	kohmoh ahgoh pahrah lyehgahr loh ahntehs pohseebleh ah...?
How many kilometres is it to...?	¿Cuántos kilómetros faltan para llegar a...?
	kwahntohs keelohmehtrohs fahltahn pahrah lyehgahr ah...?
Could you point it out on the map?	¿Podría señalarlo en el mapa?
	pohdreeah sehnyahlahrloh ehn ehl mahpah?

No sé; no soy de aquí	I don't know, I don't know my way around here
Por aquí no es	You're going the wrong way
Tiene que volver a...	You have to go back to...
Allí los carteles le indicarán	From there on just follow the signs
Vuelva a preguntar allí	When you get there, ask again

todo recto	la calle	el viaducto
straight ahead	**the street**	**the fly-over**
a la izquierda	el semáforo	el puente
left	**the traffic light**	**the bridge**
a la derecha	el túnel	el paso a nivel/las
right	**the tunnel**	barreras
doblar	el stop	**the level**
turn	**the 'give way' sign**	**crossing/the boom**
seguir	el edificio	**gates**
follow	**the building**	el cartel en
cruzar	en la esquina	dirección de...
cross	**at the corner**	**the sign pointing to...**
el cruce	el río	la flecha
the intersection	**the river**	**the arrow**

44

● **Border documents**: valid passport, visa. For car and motorbike: valid UK driving licence and registration document, insurance document, green card, UK registration plate.
Import and export specifications:
– Foreign currency: no restrictions
– Alcohol: 10 litres of spirits and 90 litres of wine. Tobacco: 800 cigarettes, 200 cigars or a kilo of tobacco. Restricted to personal consumption only.

Su pasaporte, por favor _____	Your passport, please
La tarjeta verde, por favor _____	Your green card, please
El permiso de circulación/la carta _____ gris, por favor	Your vehicle documents, please
¿Adónde va? _____	Where are you heading?
¿Cuánto tiempo piensa quedarse? _____	How long are you planning to stay?
¿Tiene algo que declarar? _____	Do you have anything to declare?
¿Puede abrir esto? _____	Open this, please

My children are entered on this passport	Mis hijos están apuntados en este pasaporte
	mees eehohs ehstahn ahpoontahdohs ehn ehsteh pahsahpohrteh
I'm travelling through _____	Estoy de paso
	ehstoy deh pahsoh
I'm going on holiday to... _____	Voy de vacaciones a...
	boy deh bahkahthyohnehs ah...
I'm on a business trip _____	He venido en viaje de negocios
	eh behneedoh ehn byahheh deh nehgohthyohs
I don't know how long I'll be staying yet	Todavía no sé cuánto tiempo me quedaré
	tohdahbeeah noh seh kwahntoh tyehmpoh meh kehdahreh
I'll be staying here for a weekend	Pienso quedarme un fin de semana
	pyehnsoh kehdahrmeh oon feen deh sehmahnah
– for a few days _____	Pienso quedarme unos días
	pyehnsoh kehdahrmeh oonohs deeahs
– for a week _____	Pienso quedarme una semana
	pyehnsoh kehdahrmeh oonah sehmahnah
– for two weeks _____	Pienso quedarme dos semanas
	pyehnsoh kehdahrmeh dohs sehmahnahs
I've got nothing to declare	No tengo nada que declarar
	noh tehngoh nahdah keh dehklahrahr
I've got...with me _____	Traigo...
	trahygoh...
– ...cartons of cigarettes _____	Traigo...cartones de cigarrillos
	trahygoh...kahrtohnehs deh theegahrreelyohs
– ...bottles of... _____	Traigo...botellas de...
	trahygoh...bohtehlyahs deh...

5

On the road

– some souvenirs _____	Traigo algunos recuerdos de viaje
	trahygoh ahlgoonohs rehkwehrdohs de
	byahheh
These are personal _____ effects	Estos son artículos personales
	ehstohs sohn ahrteekooloohs pehrsohnahlehs
These are not new _____	Estas cosas no son nuevas
	ehstahs kohsahs noh sohn nwehbahs
Here's the receipt _____	Aquí está el recibo
	ahkee ehstah ehl rehtheeboh
This is for private use _____	Esto es para uso personal
	ehstoh ehs pahrah oosoh pehrsohnahl
How much import duty _____ do I have to pay?	¿Cuánto tengo que pagar por derechos de aduana?
	kwahntoh tehngoh keh pahgahr pohr
	dehrehchohs deh ahdwahnah?
Can I go now? _____	¿Puedo seguir?
	pwehdoh sehgheer?

5 .3 Luggage

Porter! _____	¡Mozo!
	mohthoh!
Could you take this _____ luggage to...?	¿Podría llevar este equipaje a...?
	pohdreeah lyehbahr ehsteh ehkeepahheh
	_ah...?_
How much do I _____ owe you?	¿Cuánto le debo?
	kwahntoh leh dehboh?
Where can I find a _____ luggage trolley?	¿Dónde hay carritos para el equipaje?
	dohndeh ay kahrreetohs pahrah ehl
	ehkeepahheh?
Could you store this _____ luggage for me?	¿Podría dejar este equipaje en la consigna?
	pohdreeah dehhahr ehsteh ehkeepahheh
	ehn lah kohnseegnah?
Where are the luggage _____ lockers?	¿Dónde está la consigna automática?
	dohndeh ehstah lah kohnseegnah
	ahootohmahteekah?
I can't get the locker _____ open	No logro abrir la puerta de la consigna
	noh lohgroh ahbreer lah pwehrtah deh lah
	kohnseegnah
How much is it per item _____ per day?	¿Cuánto sale por bulto y por día?
	kwahntoh sahleh pohr booltoh ee pohr
	deeah?
This is not my bag/ _____ suitcase	Este/ésta no es mi bolso/mi maleta
	ehsteh/ehstah noh ehs mee bohlsoh/mee
	mahlehtah
There's one item/bag/ _____ suitcase missing still	Todavía falta un bulto/un bolso/una maleta
	tohdahbeeah fahltah oon booltoh/oon
	bohlsoh/oonah mahlehtah
My suitcase is damaged _____	Me han dañado la maleta
	meh ahn dahnyahdoh lah mahlehtah

a la derecha	ceda el paso	obras
right	**give way**	**roadworks ahead**
a la izquierda	cerrado	paso a nivel
left	**closed**	(sin barreras)
abierto	cruce peligroso	**level crossing**
open	**dangerous crossing**	(no gates)
altura máxima	curvas en ... km	paso de ganado
maximum height	**bends for...km**	**cattle crossing**
arcenes sin afirmar	despacio	peaje
soft verges	**drive slowly**	**toll**
¡atención, peligro!	desprendimientos	peatones
danger	**loose rocks**	**pedestrian crossing**
autopista de peaje	desvío	precaución
toll road	**diversion**	**caution**
autovía	dirección prohibida	prohibido aparcar
motorway	**no entry**	**no parking**
bajada peligrosa	dirección única	prohibido adelantar
steep hill	**one-way traffic**	**no overtaking**
calzada resbaladiza	encender las luces	puesto de socorro
slippery road	**switch on lights**	**first aid**
cambio de sentido	espere	salida
change of direction	**wait**	**exit**
cañada	estacionamiento	salida de camiones
animals crossing	reglamentado	**factory/works exit**
carretera comarcal	**limited parking zone**	substancias
secondary road	excepto...	peligrosas
carretera cortada	**except for...**	**dangerous**
road closed	fin de...	**substances**
carretera en mal	**end of...**	travesía peligrosa
estado	hielo	**dangerous crossing**
irregular road	**ice on road**	zona peatonal
surface	niebla	**pedestrian zone**
carretera nacional	**beware fog**	
main road		

 .5 The car

See the diagram on page 51.

● **The motorways in Spain** have been very well updated and
expanded. Tolls, however, can be expensive.

Particular traffic regulations:
maximum speed for cars:
120km/h on toll roads
110km/h on other motorways
60km/h in town centres
– give way: all traffic from the right has the right of way, except for
major roads and thoroughfares.
– towing: prohibited to private drivers.

47

● **Petrol is easily available** but rather expensive in Spain.

How many kilometres to ___ the next petrol station, please?	¿Cuántos kilómetros faltan para la próxima gasolinera? *kwahntohs keelohmehtrohs fahltahn pahrah lah prohxeemah gahsohleenehrah?*
I would like...litres of..., ___ please	Póngame...litros de..., por favor *pohngahmeh...leetrohs deh..., pohr fahbohr*
– super ___	Póngame...litros de gasolina súper *pohngahmeh...leetrohs de gahsohleenah soopehr*
– leaded ___	Póngame...litros de gasolina normal *pohngahmeh...leetrohs deh gahsohleenah nohrmahl*
– unleaded ___	Póngame...litros de gasolina sin plomo *pohngahmeh...leetrohs deh gahsohleenah seen plohmoh*
– diesel ___	Póngame...litros de gasóleo *pohngahmeh...leetrohs deh gahsohlehoh*
I would like...pesetas' ___ worth of petrol, please	Póngame gasolina por...pesetas *pohngahmeh gahsohleenah pohr...pehsehtahs*
Fill her up, please ___	Lléneme el depósito, por favor *lyehnehmeh ehl dehpohseetoh, pohr fahvohr*
Could you check...? ___	¿Podría controlar...? *pohdreeah kohntrohlahr?*
– the oil level ___	¿Podría controlar el nivel del aceite? *pohdreeah kohntrohlahr ehl neebehl dehl ahtheheeteh?*
– the tyre pressure ___	¿Podría controlar la presión de los neumáticos? *pohdreeah kohntrohlahr lah prehsyohn deh lohs nehoomahteekohs?*
Could you change the ___ oil, please?	¿Podría cambiar el aceite? *pohdreeah kahmbyahr ehl atheheeteh?*
Could you clean the ___ windows/the windscreen, please?	¿Podría limpiar los cristales/el parabrisas? *pohdreeah leempyahr lohs kreestahlehs/ehl pahrahbreesahs?*
Could you give the car ___ a wash, please?	¿Podría lavar el coche? *pohdreeah lahbahr ehl kohcheh?*

I'm having car trouble. Could you give me a hand?	Tengo una avería. ¿Podría ayudarme? *tehngoh oonah ahbehreeah. pohdreeah ahyoodahrmeh?*
I've run out of petrol	Me he quedado sin gasolina *meh eh kehdahdoh seen gahsohleenah*
I've locked the keys in the car	Me he dejado las llaves en el coche *meh eh de<u>h</u>ahdoh lahs lyabehs ehn ehl kohcheh*
The car/motorbike/ moped won't start	El coche/la moto/el ciclomotor no arranca *ehl kohcheh/lah mohtoh/ehl theeklohmohtohr noh ahrrahnkah*
Could you contact the recovery service for me, please?	¿Podría avisar al auxilio en carretera? *pohdreeah ahbeesar ahl ahooxeelyoh ehn kahrrehtehrah?*
Could you call a garage for me, please?	¿Podría llamar por teléfono a un taller mecánico? *pohdreeah lyahmahr pohr tehlehfohnoh ah oon tahlyehr mehkahneekoh?*
Could you give me a lift to...?	¿Me podría llevar a...? *meh pohdreeah lyehbahr ah...?*
– a garage/into town?	¿Me podría llevar a un taller mecánico/a la ciudad? *meh pohdreeah lyehbahr ah oon tahlyehr mehkahneekoh/ah lah thyoodahdh?*
– a phone booth?	¿Me podría llevar a una cabina de teléfonos? *meh pohdreeah lyehbahr ah oonah kahbeenah deh tehlehfohnohs?*
– an emergency phone?	¿Me podría llevar a un teléfono de emergencia? *meh pohdreeah lyehbahr ah oon tehlehfohnoh deh ehmehr<u>h</u>ehnthyah?*
Can we take my bicycle/moped?	¿Podríamos llevar la bicicleta/el ciclomotor? *pohdreeahmohs lyehbahr lah beetheeklehtah/ehl theeklohmohtohr?*
Could you tow me to a garage?	¿Podría remolcarme hasta un taller mecánico? *pohdreeah rehmohlkahrmeh ahstah oon tahlyehr mehkahneekoh?*
There's probably something wrong with...(See 5.8).	Me parece que está fallando el/la... *meh pahrehtheh keh ehstah fahlyahndoh ehl/lah...*
Can you fix it?	¿Podría arreglarlo? *pohdreeah ahrrehglahrloh?*
Could you fix my tyre?	¿Podría arreglar el neumático? *pohdreeah ahrrehglahr ehl nehoomahteekoh?*
Could you change this wheel?	¿Podría cambiar esta rueda? *pohdreeah kahmbyahr ehstah rwehdah?*

The parts of a car
(the diagram shows the numbered parts)

1	battery	la batería	*lah bahtehreeah*
2	rear light	el faro piloto	*ehl fahroh peelohtoh*
3	rear-view mirror	el retrovisor	*ehl rehtrohbeesohr*
	reversing light	la luz de marcha atrás	*lah looth deh mahrchah ahtrahs*
4	aerial	la antena	*lah ahntehnah*
	car radio	la autorradio	*lah ahootohrrahdyoh*
5	petrol tank	el depósito de gasolina	*ehl dehpohseetoh deh gahsohleenah*
	inside mirror	el espejo interior	*ehl ehspehhoh eentehreeohr*
6	sparking plugs	las bujías	*lahs booheeahs*
	fuel filter/pump	el separador de gasolina	*ehl sehpahrahdohr deh gahsohleenah*
7	wing mirror	el espejo exterior	*ehl ehspehoh ehxtehryohr*
8	bumper	el parachoques	*ehl pahrahchohkehs*
	carburettor	el carburador	*ehl kahrboorahdohr*
	crankcase	el cárter	*ehl kahrtehr*
	cylinder	el cilindro	*ehl theeleendroh*
	ignition	los contactos del ruptor	*lohs kohntahktohs dehl rooptohr*
	warning light	la luz piloto	*lah looth peelohtoh*
	dynamo	la dinamo	*lah deenahmoh*
	accelerator	el pedal del acelerador	*ehl pehdahl dehl ahtehlehrahdohr*
	handbrake	el freno de mano	*ehl frehnoh deh mahnoh*
	valve	la válvula	*lah bahlboolah*
9	silencer	el silenciador	*ehl seelehnthyahdohr*
10	boot	el maletero	*ehl mahlehtehroh*
11	headlight	el faro	*ehl fahroh*
	crank shaft	el cigueñal	*ehl theegwehnyahl*
12	air filter	el filtro de aire	*ehl feeltroh deh ayreh*
	fog lamp	la luz antiniebla trasera	*lah looth ahnteenyehblah trahsehrah*
13	engine block	el bloque motor	*ehl blohkeh mohtohr*
	camshaft	el árbol de levas	*ehl ahrbohl dehl lehbahs*
	oil filter/pump	el filtro de aceite	*ehl feeltroh deh ahtheheeteh*
	dipstick	la varilla indicadora de nivel de aceite	*lah bahreelyah eendeekahdohrah deh neebehl deh ahtheyteh*
	pedal	el pedal	*ehl pehdahl*
14	door	la portezuela	*lah pohrtehthwehlah*
15	radiator	el radiador	*ehl rahdyahdohr*
16	brake disc	el disco del freno	*ehl deeskoh dehl frehnoh*
	spare wheel	la rueda de reserva	*lah rwehdah deh rehsehrbah*
17	indicator	el intermitente	*ehl eentehrmeetehnteh*
	steering wheel	el volante	*ehl bohlahnteh*
18	windscreen wiper	el limpiaparabrisas	*ehl leempyahpahrahbreesahs*
19	shock absorbers	los amortiguadores	*lohs ahmohrteegwahdohrehs*
	sunroof	el techo corredizo	*ehl tehchoh kohrrehdeethoh*
	spoiler	el spoiler	*ehl spoheelehr*
	starter motor	el motor de arranque	*ehl mohtohr deh ahrrahnkeh*

20	steering column	el cárter de la dirección	*ehl kahrtehr deh lah deerehkthyohn*
21	exhaust pipe	el tubo de escape	*ehl tooboh deh ehskahpeh*
22	seat belt	el cinturón de seguridad	*ehl theentoorohn deh sehgooreedahdh*
	fan	el ventilador	*ehl behnteelahdohr*
23	distributor cables	los cables del distribuidor	*lohs kahblehs dehl deestreebooeedohr*
24	gear lever	la palanca de cambios	*lah pahlahnkah deh kahmbyohs*
25	windscreen	el parabrisas	*ehl pahrahbreesahs*
	water pump	la bomba de agua	*lah bohmbah deh ahgwah*
26	wheel	la rueda	*lah rwehdah*
27	hubcap	el tapacubos	*ehl tahpahkoobohs*
	piston	el émbolo	*ehl ehmbohloh*

Can you fix it so it'll get me to...?	¿Podría arreglarlo de tal manera que pueda seguir hasta...?
	pohdreeah ahrrehglahrloh deh tahl mahnehrah keh pwehdah sehgheer ahstah...?
Which garage can help me?	¿En qué taller me podrán ayudar entonces?
	ehn keh tahlyehr meh pohdrahn ahyoodahr ehntohnthehs?
When will my car/bicycle be ready?	¿Para cuándo estará mi coche/bicicleta?
	pahrah kwahndoh ehstahrah mee kohcheh/beetheeklehtah?
Can I wait for it here?	¿Puedo esperar aquí?
	pwehdoh ehspehrahr ahkee?
How much will it cost?	¿Por cuánto me va a salir?
	pohr kwahntoh meh bah ah sahleer?
Could you itemise the bill?	¿Podría especificar la cuenta?
	pohdreeah ehspehtheefeekahr lah kwehntah?
Can I have a receipt for the insurance?	¿Me podría dar un recibo para el seguro?
	meh pohdreeah dahr oon rehtheeboh pahrah ehl sehgooroh?

5 .8 The bicycle/moped

See the diagram on page 55.

● **Cycle paths** are rare in Spain. Not much consideration for bikes should be expected on the roads. The maximum speed for mopeds is 40km/h both inside and outside town centres. A helmet is compulsory.

No tengo piezas de recambio para su coche/su bicicleta	I don't have parts for your car/bicycle
Las piezas de recambio me las tienen que traer de otro sitio	I have to get the parts from somewhere else
Las piezas de recambio tengo que encargarlas	I have to order the parts
Eso llevará medio día	That'll take half a day
Eso llevará un día	That'll take a day
Eso llevará unos días	That'll take a few days
Eso llevará una semana	That'll take a week
Su coche ha quedado totalmente destruido	Your car is a write-off
Ya no se puede hacer nada para arreglarlo	It can't be repaired
El coche/la moto/el ciclomotor/la bicicleta estará para las...	The car/motor bike/moped/bicycle will be ready at... o'clock

5.9 Renting a vehicle

I'd like to rent a..._____	Quisiera alquilar un...
	keesyehrah ahlkeelahr oon...
Do I need a (special)_____ licence for that?	¿Hace falta un permiso de conducir (especial)?
	ahteh fahltah oon pehrmeesoh deh kohndootheer (ehspehthyahl)?
I'd like to rent the...for... ___	Quisiera alquilar el/la...por...
	keesyehrah ahlkeelahr ehl/lah...pohr...
– one day_____	Quisiera alquilar el/la...por un día
	keesyehrah ahlkeelahr ehl/lah...pohr oon deeah
– two days _____	Quisiera alquilar el/la...por dos días
	keesyehrah ahlkeelahr ehl/lah...pohr dohs deeahs
How much is that per_____ day/week?	¿Cuánto sale por día/semana?
	kwahntoh sahleh pohr deeah/pohr sehmahnah?
How much is the _____ deposit?	¿Cuánto es la fianza?
	kwahntoh ehs lah fyahnthah?
Could I have a receipt _____ for the deposit?	¿Me podría dar un recibo por el pago de la fianza?
	meh pohdreeah dahr oon rehtheeboh pohr ehl pahgoh deh lah fyahnthah?
How much is the _____ surcharge per kilometre?	¿Cuánto hay que pagar extra por kilómetro?
	kwahntoh ay keh pahgahr ehxtrah pohr keelohmehtroh?
Does that include _____ petrol?	¿Está incluida la gasolina?
	ehstah eenklooeedah lah gahsohleenah?
Does that include _____ insurance?	¿Está incluido el seguro?
	ehstah eenklooeedoh ehl sehgooroh?
What time can I pick_____ the...up tomorrow?	¿A qué hora puedo pasar mañana a buscar el/la...?
	ah keh ohrah pwehdoh pahsahr mahnyahnah ah booskahr ehl/lah...?
When does the...have _____ to be back?	¿A qué hora tengo que devolver el/la...?
	ah keh ohrah tehngoh keh dehbohlbehr ehl/lah...?
Where's the petrol tank? ___	¿Dónde está el depósito de gasolina?
	dohndeh ehstah ehl dehpohseetoh deh gahsohleenah?
What sort of fuel does _____ it take?	¿Qué tipo de combustible hay que echarle?
	keh teepoh deh kohmboosteebleh ay keh ehchahrleh?

5.10 Hitchhiking

Where are you heading? ___	¿Adónde va?
	ahdohndeh bah?
Can I come along? _____	¿Me podría llevar?
	meh pohdreeah lyehbahr?
Can my boyfriend/ _____ girlfriend come too?	¿Podría llevar también a mi amigo/amiga?
	pohdreeah lyehbahr tahmbyehn ah mee ahmeegoh/ahmeegah?

The parts of a bicycle

(the diagram shows the numbered parts)

1 rear lamp	el piloto	*ehl peelohtoh*
2 rear wheel	la rueda trasera	*lah rwehdah trahsehrah*
3 (luggage) carrier	el portaequipajes	*ehl pohrtahehkeepah<u>h</u>ehs*
4 bicycle fork	la cabeza	*lah kahbehthah*
5 bell	el timbre	*ehl teembreh*
inner tube	la cámara	*lah kahmahrah*
tyre	el neumático/la cubierta	*ehl nehoomahteekoh/lah koobyehrtah*
6 crank	la biela	*lah byehlah*
7 gear change	el cambio de velocidades	*ehl kahmbyoh deh behlotheedahdehs*
wire	el hilo	*ehl eeloh*
dynamo	la dinamo	*lah deenahmoh*
bicycle trailer	el remolque de bicicleta	*ehl rehmohlkeh deh beetheeklehtah*
frame	el cuadro	*ehl kwahdroh*
8 dress guard	el guardafaldas	*ehl gwardahfahldahs*
9 chain	la cadena de rodillos	*lah kahdehnah deh rohdeelyohs*
chain guard	el cubrecadena/el cárter	*ehl koobrehkahdehnah/ehl kahrtehr*
chain lock	la cadena antirrobo	*lah kahdehnah ahnteerrohboh*
milometer	el contador kilométrico	*ehl kohntahdohr keelohmehtreekoh*
child's seat	el sillín para niños	*ehl seelyeen pahrah neenyohs*
10 headlamp	el faro	*ehl fahroh*
bulb	la bombilla	*lah bohmbeelyah*
11 pedal	el pedal	*ehl pehdahl*
12 pump	la bombilla	*lah bohmbeelyah*
13 reflector	el cristal reflectante	*ehl kreestahl rehflehktahnteh*
14 brake pad	la zapatilla del freno	*lah thahpahteelyah dehl frehnoh*
15 brake cable	el cable del freno	*ehl kahbleh dehl frehnoh*
16 ring lock	la cerradura	*lah thehrrahdoorah*
17 carrier straps	las bandas elásticas	*lahs bahndahs ehlahsteekahs*
tachometer		
18 spoke	el velocímetro	*ehl behlohtheemehtroh*
19 mudguard	el radio/el rayo	*ehl rahdyoh/ehl rahyoh*
20 handlebar	el guardabarros	*ehl gwahrdahbahrrohs*
21 chain wheel	el manillar	*ehl mahneelyahr*
toe clip	el piñón	*ehl peenyohn*
22 crank axle	el calapiés	*ehl kahlahpyehs*
drum brake	el eje del cigueñal	*ehl ehhe dehl theegwehnyal*
rim	el freno de tambor	*ehl frehnoh deh tahmbohr*
23 tube	la llanta	*lah lyahntah*
24 valve	la válvula	*lah bahlboolah*
valve tube	el tubo de la válvula	*ehl tooboh deh lah bahlboolah*

25 gear cable	el cable de velocidades	*ehl kahbleh deh behlohtheedahdehs*
26 fork	la horquilla	*lah ohrkeelyah*
27 front wheel	la rueda delantera	*lah rwehdah dehlahntehrah*
28 seat	el sillín	*el seelyeen*

I'm trying to get to... _____ Voy a...
boy ah...

Is that on the way to...? _____ ¿Eso está camino de...?
ehsoh ehstah kahmeenoh deh...?

Could you drop _____ ¿Me podría dejar...?
me off...? *meh pohdreeah dehhahr...?*

– here? _____ ¿Me podría dejar aquí mismo?
meh pohdreeah dehhahr ahkee meesmoh?

– at the...exit? _____ ¿Me podría dejar en la salida de...?
meh pohdreeah dehhahr ehn lah sahleedah deh...?

– in the centre? _____ ¿Me podría dejar en el centro?
meh pohdreeah dehhahr ehn ehl thehntroh?

– at the next roundabout? ___ ¿Me podría dejar en la próxima rotonda?
meh pohdreeah dehhahr ehn lah prohxeemah rohtohndah?

Could you stop here, _____ ¿Podría pararse aquí?
please? *pohdreeah pahrahrseh ahkee?*

I'd like to get out here _____ Quisiera bajarme aquí
keesyehrah bahhahrmeh ahkee

Thanks for the lift _____ Gracias por llevarme
grahthyahs pohr lyehbahrmeh

6

Public transport

6 Public transport

6.1 In general

● **The rail network** has been substantially overhauled and expanded and there is now a good, fast service available with the Talgo and Ave in the south. These trains require payment of a supplement and it is advisable to reserve seats in advance, at the station or at travel agencies. Tickets for buses and the metro can be bought at an *estanco*, as well as metro stations.

Announcements

El tren [de las 10:40] con destino a..., ..., saldrá con (unos)...minutos de retraso	The [10:40] train to...has been delayed by 15 minutes
Por la vía 5 entrará el tren _____ [de las 10:40] con destino a.../ procedente de...	The train now arriving at platform 5 is the [10:40] train to .../from...
En la vía 5 está por partir el tren _____ [de las 10:40]...	The [10:40] train to...is about to leave from platform 5
Su atención, por favor _____ Manténganseselejos de la vía; un tren intercity pasará por la plataforma...	Attention please! Keep your distance from the rail track, an intercity train will pass on platform...
Nos estamos aproximando a la _____ estación de...	We're now approaching...

Where does this train go to?	¿Adónde va este tren? *ahdohndeh bah ehsteh trehn?*
Does this boat go to...?	¿Este barco va a...? *ehsteh bahrkoh bah ah...?*
Can I take this bus to...?	¿Puedo coger este autobús para ir a...? *pwehdoh kohhehr ehsteh ahootohboos pahrah eer ah...?*
Does this train stop at...?	¿Este tren para en...? *ehsteh trehn pahrah ehn...?*
Is this seat taken/free /reserved?	¿Está ocupado/libre/reservado este asiento? *ehstah ohkoopahdoh/leebreh/rehsehrbahdoh ehsteh ahsyehntoh?*
I've booked...	He reservado... *he rehsehrbahdoh...*
Could you tell me where I have to get off for...?	¿Me podría decir dónde me tengo que bajar para ir a...? *meh pohdreeah dehtheer dohndeh meh tehngoh keh bahhar pahrah eer ah...?*
Could you let me know when we get to...?	¿Me podría avisar cuando lleguemos a...? *meh pohdreeah ahbeesahr kwahndoh lyehghehmohs ah...?*
Could you stop at the next stop, please?	La próxima parada, por favor *lah prohxeemah pahrahdah pohr fahbohr*

Where are we now? _____	¿Dónde estamos?
	dohndeh ehstahmohs?
Do I have to get off here? __	¿Tengo que bajarme aquí?
	tehngoh keh bah<u>h</u>ahrmeh ahkee?
Have we already _____ passed...?	¿Ya hemos pasado...?
	yah ehmohs pahsahdoh...?
How long have I been _____ asleep?	¿Cuánto tiempo he dormido?
	kwahntoh tyehmpoh eh dohrmeedoh?
How long does... _____ stop here?	¿Cuánto tiempo se queda aquí...?
	kwahntoh tyehmpoh seh kehdah ahkee?
Can I come back on the ____ same ticket?	¿Este billete me sirve para volver?
	ehsteh beelyehteh meh seerbeh pahrah bohlbehr?
Can I change on this_____ ticket?	¿Se puede hacer trasbordo con este billete?
	seh pwehdeh ahthehr trahsbohrdoh kohn ehsteh beelyehteh?
How long is this ticket _____ valid for?	¿Hasta cuándo es válido este billete?
	ahstah kwahndoh ehs bahleedoh ehsteh beelyehteh
How much is the _____ supplement for the Talgo/Ave (high speed train)?	¿Cuánto vale el suplemento para el Talgo/el Ave?
	kwahntoh bahleh ehl sooplehmehntoh pahrah ehl tahlgoh/ehl ahbeh?

6 .2 Questions to passengers

Ticket types

¿Primera o segunda clase? _____	First or second class?
¿Billete de ida o de ida y vuelta? _____	Single or return?
¿Fumadores o no fumadores? _____	Smoking or non-smoking?
¿Ventanilla o pasillo?_____	Window or aisle?
¿Adelante o atrás? _____	Front or back?
¿Asiento o litera? _____	Seat or couchette?
¿Arriba, en el medio o abajo?_____	Top, middle or bottom?
¿Clase turista o preferente?_____	Tourist class or business class?
¿Camarote o butaca? _____	Cabin or seat?
¿Individual o doble? _____	Single or double?
¿Cuántas personas viajan? _____	How many are travelling?

Destination

¿Adónde quiere ir?		Where are you travelling?
¿Qué día sale?		When are you leaving?
Su...sale a las...		Your...leaves at...
Tiene que hacer trasbordo		You have to change trains
Tiene que bajarse en...		You have to get off at...
Tiene que pasar por...		You have to travel via...
El viaje de ida es el día...		The outward journey is on...
El viaje de vuelta es el día...		The return journey is on...
Tiene que embarcar a las...a más tardar		You have to be on board by...

Inside the vehicle

Billetes, por favor		Your ticket, please
Su reserva, por favor		Your reservation, please
Su pasaporte, por favor		Your passport, please
Se ha equivocado de asiento		You're in the wrong seat
Se ha equivocado de...		You're on/in the wrong...
Este asiento está reservado		This seat is reserved
Tiene que pagar un suplemento		You'll have to pay a supplement
El...tiene un retraso de...minutos		The...has been delayed by...minutes

6 .3 Tickets

Where can I...?	¿Dónde...?
	dohndeh...?
– buy a ticket?	¿Dónde se compran los billetes?
	dohndeh seh kohmprahn lohs beelyehtehs?
– make a reservation?	¿Dónde se hacen las reservas?
	dohndeh seh ahtehn lahs rehsehrbahs?
– book a flight?	¿Dónde puedo hacer una reserva para un vuelo?
	dohndeh pwehdoh ahtehr oonah rehsehrbah pahrah oon bwehloh?
Could I have a...to..., please?	Quiero un/una...a...
	kyehroh oon/oonah...ah...
– a single	Quiero un billete de ida a...
	kyehroh oon beelyehteh deh eedah ah...
– a return	Quiero un billete de ida y vuelta a...
	kyehroh oon beelyehteh deh eedah ee bwehltah ah...
first class	en primera clase
	ehn preemehrah klahseh
second class	en segunda clase
	ehn sehgoondah klahseh

tourist class _____	en clase turista *ehn klahseh tooreestah*
business class _____	en clase preferente *ehn klahseh prehfehrehnteh*
I'd like to book a _____ seat/couchette/cabin	Quisiera reservar un asiento/una litera/un camarote *keesyehrah rehsehrbahr oon ahsyehntoh/oonah leetehrah/oon kahmahrohteh*
I'd like to book a berth _____ in the sleeping car	Quisiera reservar una plaza en un coche cama *keesyehrah rehsehrbahr oonah plahthah ehn oon kohcheh kahmah*
top/middle/bottom _____	arriba/en el medio/abajo *ahrreebah/ehn ehl mehdyoh/ahbah<u>h</u>oh*
smoking/no smoking _____	fumadores/no fumadores *foomahdohrehs/noh foomahdohrehs*
by the window _____	ventanilla *behntahneelyah*
single/double _____	individual/doble *eendeebeedwahl/dohbleh*
at the front/back _____	adelante/atrás *ahdehlahnteh/ahtrahs*
There are...of us _____	Somos...personas *sohmohs...pehrsohnahs*
a car _____	un coche *oon kohcheh*
a caravan _____	una caravana *oonah kahrahbahnah*
...bicycles _____	...bicicletas *...beetheeklehtahs*
Do you also have...? _____	¿Tienen...? *tyehnehn...?*
– season tickets? _____	¿Tienen billetes para varios viajes? *tyehnen beelyehtehs pahrah bahryohs byahhehs?*
– weekly tickets? _____	¿Tienen abonos semanales? *tyehnehn ahbohnohs sehmahnahlehs?*
– monthly season _____ tickets?	¿Tienen abonos mensuales? *tyehnehn ahbohnohs mehnswahlehs?*

6 .4 Information

Where's-? _____	¿Dónde hay...? *dohndeh ay...?*
Where's the information _____ desk?	¿Dónde está la oficina de información? *dohndeh ehstah lah ohfeetheenah deh eenfohrmahthyohn?*
Where can I find a _____ timetable?	¿Dónde hay un horario? *dohndeh ay oon ohrahryoh?*
Where's the...desk? _____	¿Dónde está el mostrador de...? *dohndeh ehstah ehl mohstrahdohr deh...?*
Do you have a city map _____ with the bus/the underground routes on it?	¿Tendría un plano de la ciudad con la red de autobuses/metro? *tehndreeah oon plahnoh deh lah thyoodahdh kohn lah rehth deh ahootohboosehs/mehtroh?*

Do you have a _____ timetable?	¿Tendría un horario?
	tehndreeah oon ohrahryoh?
I'd like to confirm/_____ cancel/change my booking for/trip to...	Quisiera confirmar/cancelar/cambiar mi reserva/mi viaje a...
	keesyehrah kohnfeermahr/kahnthehlahr/kahmbyahr mee rehsehrbah/mee byahheh ah...
Will I get my money _____ back?	¿Me devuelven el dinero?
	meh dehbwehlbehn ehl deenehroh?
I want to go to... _____ How do I get there? (What's the quickest way there?)	Tengo que ir a...¿Cómo hago para llegar (lo más rápido posible)?
	tehngoh keh eer ah...kohmoh ahgoh pahrah lyehgahr(loh mahs rahpeedoh pohseebleh)?
How much is a _____ single/return to...?	¿Cuánto vale un billete de ida/de ida y vuelta a...?
	kwahntoh bahleh oon beelyehteh deh eedah ee eedah ee bwehltah ah...?
Do I have to pay a _____ supplement?	¿Tengo que pagar algún suplemento?
	tehngoh keh pahgahr ahlgoon sooplehmehntoh?
Can I interrupt my _____ journey with this ticket?	¿Con este billete puedo hacer una parada intermedia?
	kohn ehsteh beelyehteh pwehdoh ahthehr oonah pahrahdah eentehrmehdyah?
How much luggage _____ am I allowed?	¿Cuánto equipaje puedo llevar?
	kwahntoh ehkeepahheh pwehdoh lyebahr?
Can I send my luggage _____ in advance?	¿Puedo enviar mi equipaje por anticipado?
	pwehdoh ehnbeeahr mee ehkeepahheh pohr ahnteetheepahdoh?
Does this...travel direct? _____	¿Este...va directo?
	ehsteh...bah deerehktoh?
Do I have to change? _____ Where?	¿Tengo que hacer trasbordo? ¿Dónde?
	tehngoh keh ahthehr trahsbohrdoh? dohndeh?
Will there be any _____ stopovers?	¿Habrá escalas?
	ahbrah ehskahlahs?
Does the boat call in at _____ any ports on the way?	¿El barco hace alguna escala?
	ehl bahrkoh ahtheh ahlgoonah ehskahlah?
Does the train/_____ bus stop at...?	¿Este tren/este autobús para en...?
	ehsteh trehn/ehsteh ahootohboos pahrah ehn...?
Where should I get off? _____	¿Dónde me tengo que bajar?
	dohndeh meh tehngoh keh bahhahr?
Is there a connection _____ to...?	¿Hay enlace para...?
	ay ehnlahtheh pahrah...?
How long do I have to _____ wait?	¿Cuánto tengo que esperar?
	kwahntoh tehngoh keh ehspehrahr?
When does...leave? _____	¿Cuándo sale...?
	kwahndoh sahleh...?
What time does the _____ first/next/last...leave?	¿A qué hora sale el primer/próximo/último...?
	ah keh ohrah sahleh ehl preemehr/prohxeemoh/oolteemoh...?
How long does...take? _____	¿Cuánto tarda...en llegar?
	kwahntoh tahrdah...ehn lyehgahr?

What time does...arrive in...?	¿A qué hora llega...a...? *ah keh ohrah lyegah...ah...?*
Where does the...to...leave from?	¿De dónde sale el...a...? *deh dohndeh sahleh ehl...ah...?*
Is this...to...?	¿Este es...a...? *ehsteh ehs...ah...?*

.5 Aeroplanes

● **On arrival** at a Spanish airport, you will find the following signs:

llegadas arrivals	salidas departures

.6 Trains

● **The rail network** is very extensive, run by the RENFE (Red Nacional de Ferrocarriles Españoles). Some local trains are still rather slow so it is preferable to stipulate Talgo or Rápido when buying tickets. During the summer and before public holidays it is advisable to buy train tickets well in advance. Porters are few and far between.

.7 Taxis

● **There are plenty of taxis** in most cities. Supplements are payable for luggage and travel to stations or airports. It is advisable to inquire about the price in advance and make sure that you are hiring a city taxi.

libre for hire	ocupado booked	parada de taxis taxi rank

Taxi!	¡Taxi! *tahxee!*
Could you get me a taxi, please?	¿Me podría llamar un taxi? *meh pohdreeah lyahmahr oon tahksee?*
Where can I find a taxi around here?	¿Dónde se puede coger un taxi por aquí? *dohndeh seh pwehdeh kohhehr oon tahxee pohr ahkee?*
Could you take me to..., please?	A..., por favor *ah..., pohr fahbohr*
– this address	A esta dirección, por favor *ah ehstah deerehkthyohn, pohr fahbohr*
– the...hotel	Al hotel..., por favor *ahl ohtehl..., pohr fahbohr*
– the town/city centre	Al centro, por favor *ahl thehntroh, pohr fahbohr*
– the station	A la estación, por favor *ah lah ehstahthyohn, pohr fahbohr*
– the airport	Al aeropuerto, por favor *ahl ahehrohpwehrtoh, pohr fahbohr*

How much is the ___ trip to...?	¿Cuánto sale el recorrido hasta...?
	kwahntoh sahleh ehl rehkohrreedoh ahstah...?
How far is it to...? ___	¿Cuánto es hasta...?
	kwahntoh ehs ahstah...?
Could you turn on the ___ meter, please?	¿Podría poner en marcha el taxímetro?
	pohdreeah pohnehr ehn mahrchah ehl tahxeemehtroh?
I'm in a hurry ___	Llevo prisa
	lyehboh preesah
Could you speed up/slow ___ down a little?	¿Podría ir más rápido/más despacio?
	pohdreeah eer mahs rahpeedoh/mahs dehspathyoh?
Could you take a ___ different route?	¿Podría ir por otro camino?
	pohdreeah eer pohr ohtroh kahmeenoh?
I'd like to get out here, ___ please	Déjeme aquí
	dehhehmeh ahkee
You have to go...here ___	Siga...aquí
	seegah...ahkee
You have to go straight ___ on here	Siga todo recto aquí
	seegah tohdoh rehktoh akee
You have to turn left ___ here	Doble a la izquierda aquí
	dohbleh ah lah eethkyehrdah ahkee
You have to turn right ___ here	Dobleh a la derecha aquí
	dohbleh ah lah dehrehchah ahkee
This is it ___	Es aquí
	ehs ahkee
Could you wait a minute ___ for me, please?	Espéreme un momentito, por favor
	ehspehrehmeh oon mohmehnteetoh, pohr fahbohr

Overnight accommodation

Overnight accommodation

7 .1 General

● **There is great variety** in overnight accommodation in Spain.
It is advisable to book (and send confirmation) in advance.
Hotel: stars indicate the degree of comfort; from five stars, the most
luxurious, to one star, very basic. Most hotels offer *pensión completa*
(full board) or *media pensión* (half board).
Parador: Mainly, but not always, luxurious hotels in converted
castles or palaces in exceptional areas. These are very popular and
have to be booked very well in advance, but are well worth the visit.
They are under government supervision.
Hostal: Family run businesses for the most part, with one to three
stars. They do not always provide breakfast, but are clean and can be
very well situated.
Albergue: usually country inns.
Albergue de juventud: restricted to members of the international Youth
Hostels Association.
Camping: a list of sites can be found at any Tourist Office.

¿Cuánto tiempo piensa quedarse?	How long will you be staying?
Rellene este formulario, por favor	Fill in this form, please
¿Me permite su pasaporte?	Could I see your passport?
Tiene que pagar una fianza	I'll need a deposit
Tiene que pagar por adelantado	You'll have to pay in advance

My name's...I've made a reservation over the phone/by mail	Me llamo...He reservado una habitación por teléfono/por carta *meh lyahmoh...eh rehsehrbahdoh oonah ahbeetahthyohn pohr tehlehfohnoh/pohr kahrtah*
How much is it per night/week/ month?	¿Cuánto sale por noche/semana/mes? *kwahntoh sahleh pohr nohcheh/sehmahnah/mehs?*
We'll be staying at least...nights/weeks	Pensamos quedarnos al menos...noches/semanas *pehnsahmohs kehdahrnohs ahl mehnohs...nohchehs/sehmahnahs*
We don't know yet	Todavía no lo sabemos exactamente *tohdahbeeah noh loh sahbehmohs ehxahktahmehnte*
Do you allow pets (cats/dogs)?	¿Están permitidos los animales domésticos (perros/gatos)? *ehstahn pehrmeeteedohs lohs ahneemahlehs dohmehsteekohs(pehrrohs/gahtohs)?*
What time does the gate/door open/close?	¿A qué hora cierran/abren la verja/la puerta de entrada? *ah keh ohrah thyehrrahn/ahbrehn lah behrhah/lah pwehrtah deh ehntrahdah?*

Could you get me _____ a taxi, please?	¿Podría llamar un taxi?
	pohdreeah lyahmahr oon tahxee?
Is there any mail _____ for me?	¿Hay carta para mí?
	ay kahrtah pahrah mee?

7 .2 Camping

See the diagram on page 69.

Puede elegir el sitio usted mismo _____	You can pick your own site
El sitio se lo asignamos nosotros _____	You'll be allocated a site
Este es el número de su _____ emplazamiento	This is your site number
Por favor pegue esto en el parabrisas ___ del coche	Stick this on your car, please
No pierda esta tarjeta _____	Please don't lose this card

Where's the manager? _____	¿Dónde está el encargado?
	dohndeh ehstah ehl ehnkahrgahdoh?
Are we allowed to _____ camp here?	¿Podemos acampar aquí?
	pohdehmohs ahkahmpahr ahkee?
There are...of us and _____ ...tents	Somos...personas y...tiendas
	sohmohs...pehrsohnahs ee...tyehndahs
Can we pick our _____ own site?	¿Podemos elegir el sitio nosotros mismos?
	pohdehmohs ehlehheer ehl seetyoh nohsohtrohs meesmohs?
Do you have a quiet _____ spot for us?	¿Nos podría dar un sitio tranquilo?
	nohs pohdreeah dahr oon seetyoh trahnkeeloh?
Do you have any other ___ sites available?	¿No tiene otro sitio libre?
	noh tyehneh ohtroh seetyoh leebreh?
It's too windy/sunny/ _____ shady here.	Hay mucho viento/mucho sol/mucha sombra
	ay moochoh byehntoh/moochoh sohl/moochah sohmbrah
It's too crowded here _____	Hay mucha gente
	ay moochah hehnteh
The ground's too _____ hard/uneven	El suelo es muy duro/muy desigual
	ehl swehloh ehs mwee dooroh/mwee dehseegwahl
Do you have a level _____ spot for the camper/caravan/folding caravan?	¿Tiene un sitio plano para el autocaravana/la caravana/el remolque tienda?
	tyehneh oon seetyoh plahnoh pahrah ehl ahootohkahrahbahnah/lah kahrahbahnah/ehl rehmohlkeh-tyehndah?
Could we have _____ adjoining sites?	¿Tiene dos plazas juntas?
	tyehneh dohs plahthahs hoontahs?
Can we park the car _____ next to the tent?	¿Podemos aparcar el coche junto a la tienda?
	pohdehmohs ahpahrkahr ehl kohcheh hoontoh ah lah tyehndah?

Camping equipment
(the diagram shows the numbered parts)

	luggage space	el compartimiento de equipaje	*ehl kohmpahrteemyehntoh de ehkeepahhheh*
	can opener	el abrelatas	*ehl ahbrehlahtahs*
	butane gas bottle	la bombona (de gas butano)	*lah bohmbohnah (deh gahs bootahnoh)*
1	pannier	la ciclobolsa	*lah theeklohbohlsah*
2	gas cooker	el hornillo de gas	*ehl ohrneelyoh deh gahs*
3	groundsheet	la lona del suelo	*lah lohnah dehl swehloh*
	mallet	el martillo	*ehl mahrteelyoh*
	hammock	la hamaca	*lah ahmahkah*
4	jerry can	el bidón	*ehl beedohn*
	campfire	la fogata	*lah fohgahtah*
5	folding chair	la silla plegable	*lah seelyah plehgahbleh*
6	insulated picnic box	la nevera portátil/la bolsa nevera	*lah nehbehrah pohrtahteel/lah bohlsah nehbehrah*
	ice pack	el acumulador	*ehl akoomoolahdohr*
	compass	la brújula	*lah broohoolah*
	wick	la mecha	*lah mehchah*
	corkscrew	el sacacorchos	*ehl sahkahkohrchohs*
7	airbed	el colchón neumático	*ehl kohlchohn nehoomahteekoh*
8	airbed plug	el taponcito de la válvula del colchón	*ehl tahpohntheetoh deh lah bahlboolah dehl kohlchohn*
	pump	la bomba neumática	*lah bohmbah nehoomahteekah*
9	awning	el tejadillo	*ehl tehhahdeelyoh*
10	karimat	la esterilla	*lah ehstehreelyah*
11	pan	la olla	*lah ohlyah*
12	pan handle	el mango de la olla	*ehl mahngoh deh lah ohlyah*
	primus stove	el hornillo de querosén	*ehl ohrneelyoh deh kehrohsehn*
	zip	la cremallera	*lah krehmalyehrah*
13	backpack	la mochila	*lah mohcheelah*
14	guy rope	el viento	*ehl byehntoh*
	sleeping bag	el saco de dormir	*ehl sahkoh deh dohrmeer*
15	storm lantern	el farol de tormentas	*ehl fahrohl deh tohrmehntahs*
	camp bed	el catre (de tijera)	*ehl kahtreh (deh teehehrah)*
	table	la mesa	*lah mehsah*
16	tent	la tienda	*lah tyehndah*
17	tent peg	la estaca	*lah ehstakah*
18	tent pole	el palo de tienda	*ehl pahloh deh tyehndah*
	vacuum flask	el termo	*ehl tehrmoh*
19	water bottle	la cantimplora	*lah kahnteemplohrah*
	clothes peg	la pinza	*lah peenthah*
	clothes line	la cuerda de tender ropa	*lah kwehrdah deh tehndehr rohpah*
	windbreak	el paravientos/el paraván	*ehl pahrahbyehntohs/ehl pahrahbahn*
20	torch	la linterna de bolsillo	*lah leentehrnah deh bohlseelyoh*
	pocket knife	la navaja	*lah nahbahhah*

How much is it per person/tent/caravan/car?	¿Cuánto sale por persona/tienda/caravana/coche?
	kwahntoh sahleh pohr pehrsohnah/tyehndah/ kahrahbahnah/kohcheh?
Are there any...?	¿Hay...?
	ay...?
– any hot showers?	¿Hay duchas con agua caliente?
	ay doochahs kohn ahgwah kahlyehnteh?
– washing machines?	¿Hay lavadoras?
	ay lahbahdohrahs?
Is there a...on the site?	¿En este camping hay...?
	ehn ehsteh kahmpeen ay...?
Is there a children's play area on the site?	¿En este camping hay un sitio para que jueguen los niños?
	ehn ehsteh kahmpeen ay oon seetyoh pahrah keh hwehghehn lohs neenyohs?
Are there covered cooking facilities on the site?	¿En este camping hay un sitio cubierto para cocinar?
	ehn ehsteh kahmpeen ay oon seetyoh koobyehrtoh pahrah kohtheenahr?
Can I rent a safe here?	¿Tienen caja fuerte para alquilar?
	tyehnehn kahhah fwehrteh pahrah ahlkeelahr?
Are we allowed to barbecue here?	¿Se pueden hacer barbacoas?
	seh pwehdehn ahtehr bahrbahkohahs?
Are there any power points?	¿Hay tomas de corriente eléctrica?
	ay tohmahs deh kohrryehnteh ehlehktreekah?
Is there drinking water?	¿Hay agua potable?
	ay ahgwah pohtahbleh?
When's the rubbish collected?	¿Cuándo pasan a recoger la basura?
	kwahndoh pahsahn ah rehkohhehr lah bahsoorah?
Do you sell gas bottles (butane gas/propane gas)?	¿Venden bombonas de gas (butano/propano)?
	behndehn bohmbohnahs deh gahs(bootahnoh/prohpahnoh)?

Overnight accommodation

7.3 Hotel/B&B/apartment/holiday house

Do you have a single/double room available?	¿Le queda alguna habitación individual/doble?
	leh kehdah ahlgoonah ahbeetahthyohn eendeebeedwahl/dohbleh?
per person/per room	por persona/por habitación
	pohr pehrsohnah/pohr ahbeetahthyohn
Does that include breakfast/lunch/dinner?	¿Incluye desayuno/comida/cena?
	eenklooyeh dehsahyoonoh/kohmeedah/thehnah?
Could we have two adjoining rooms?	¿Nos puede dar dos habitaciones una al lado de la otra?
	nohs pwehdeh dahr dohs ahbeetahthyohnehs oonah ahl lahdoh deh lah ohtrah?
with/without toilet/bath/shower	con/sin lavabo propio/baño propio/ducha propia
	kohn/seen lahbahboh prohpyoh/bahnyoh prohpyo/doochah prohpyah?

(not) facing the street	que (no) dé a la calle
	keh (noh) deh ah lah kahlyeh
with/without a view of the sea	con/sin vista al mar
	kohn/seen beestah ahl mahr
Is there...in the hotel?	¿El hotel tiene...?
	ehl ohtehl tyehneh...?
Is there a lift in the hotel?	¿El hotel tiene ascensor?
	ehl ohtehl tyehneh ahsthehnsohr?
Do you have room service?	¿El hotel tiene servicio de habitación?
	ehl ohtehl tyehneh sehrbeethyoh deh ahbeetahthyohn?

Tiene lavabo y ducha en el mismo piso/en su habitación	You can find the toilet and shower on the same floor/en suite
Por aquí, por favor	This way, please
Su habitación está en el...piso; es la número...	Your room is on the...floor, number...

Could I see the room?	¿Puedo ver la habitación?
	pwehdoh behr lah ahbeetahthyohn?
I'll take this room	Me quedo con esta habitación
	meh kehdoh kohn ehstah abeetathyohn
We don't like this one	Esta no nos gusta
	ehstah noh nohs goostah
Do you have a larger/less expensive room?	¿Tiene una habitación más grande/más barata?
	tyehneh oonah ahbeetathyohn mahs grahnde/mahs bahrahtah?
Could you put in a cot?	¿Puede agregar una cuna?
	pwehde ahgrehgahr oonah koonah?
What time's breakfast?	¿A qué hora es el desayuno?
	ah keh ohrah ehs ehl dehsahyoonoh?
Where's the dining room?	¿Dónde está el comedor?
	dohndeh ehstah ehl kohmehdohr?
Can I have breakfast in my room?	¿Me pueden traer el desayuno a la habitación?
	meh pwehdehn trahehr ehl dehsahyoonoh ah lah ahbeetahthyohn?
Where's the emergency exit/fire escape?	¿Dónde está la salida de emergencia/la escalera de incendios?
	dohndeh ehstah lah sahleedah deh ehmehrhehnthyah/lah ehskahlehrah de eenthehndyohs?
Where can I park my car (safely)?	¿Dónde hay un sitio (seguro) para aparcar el coche?
	dohndeh ay oon seetyoh sehgooroh pahrah ahpahrkahr ehl kohcheh?
The key to room..., please	La llave de la habitación..., por favor
	lah lyahbeh deh lah ahbeetahthyohn..., pohr fahbohr
Could you put this in the safe, please?	¿Podría dejar esto en la caja fuerte?
	pohdreeah dehhahr ehstoh ehn lah cahhah fwehrteh?

7

Overnight accommodation

71

Could you wake me _____ at...tomorrow?	¿Me podría despertar mañana a las...? _meh pohdreeah dehspehrtahr mahnyahnah ah lahs...?_
Could you find a _____ babysitter for me?	¿Me podría conseguir una niñera para el bebé? _meh pohdreeah kohnsehgueer oonah neenyehrah pahrah ehl behbeh?_
Could I have an extra_____ blanket?	¿Tendría una manta extra? _tehndreeah oonah mahntah ehxtrah?_
What days do the _____ cleaners come in?	¿Qué días limpian la habitación? _keh deeahs leempyahn lah ahbeetahthyohn?_
When are the sheets/ _____ towels/tea towels changed?	¿Cuándo cambian las sábanas/las toallas/los paños de cocina? _kwahndoh kahmbyahn lahs sahbahnahs/lahs tohahlyahs/lohs pahnyohs deh kohtheenah?_

.4 Complaints

We can't sleep for _____ the noise	No podemos dormir por el ruido _noh pohdehmohs dohrmeer pohr ehl rweedoh_
Could you turn the _____ radio down, please?	¿Podría bajar el volumen de la radio? _pohdreeah bahhahr ehl vohloomehn deh lah rahdyoh?_
We're out of toilet paper ___	Se ha acabado el papel higiénico. _seh ah ahkahbahdoh ehl pahpehl eehyehneekoh_
There aren't any.../ _____ there's not enough...	No hay.../no hay suficientes... _noh ay.../noh ay soofeethyehntehs..._
The bed linen's dirty_____	La ropa de cama está sucia _lah rohpah deh kahmah ehstah soothyah_
The room hasn't been _____ cleaned.	No han limpiado la habitación _noh ahn leempyahdoh lah ahbeetahthyohn_
The kitchen is not clean___	La cocina no está limpia _lah kohtheenah noh ehstah leempyah_
The kitchen utensils are___ dirty	Los utensilios de cocina están sucios _lohs ootehnseelyohs deh kohtheenah ehstahn soothyohs_
The heater's not_____ working	La calefacción no funciona _lah kahlehfahkthyohn noh foonthyohnah_
There's no (hot) _____ water/electricity	No hay agua (caliente)/electricidad _noh ay ahgwah(kahlyehnteh)/ehlehktreetheedahdh_
...is broken_____	...está estropeado _...ehstah ehstrohpehahdoh_
Could you have that _____ seen to?	¿Podrían hacerlo ver? _pohdreeahn ahthehrloh behr?_
Could I have another _____ room/site?	¿Tendría otra habitación/sitio para la tienda? _tehndreeah ohtrah abeetahthyohn/seetyoh pahrah lah tyehndah?_
The bed creaks terribly ___	La cama hace mucho ruido _lah kahmah ahtheh moochoh rweedoh_
The bed sags _____	La cama es demasiado blanda _lah kahmah ehs dehmahsyahdoh blahndah_

Overnight accommodation

There are bugs/insects_____ in our room	Hay muchos bichos/insectos en nuestra habitación
	ay moochohs beechohs/eensehktohs ehn nooehstrah ahbeetahthyohn
This place is full_____ of mosquitos	Está lleno de mosquitos
	ehstah lyehnoh deh mohskeetohs
– cockroaches_____	Está lleno de cucarachas
	ehstah lyehnoh deh kookahrahchahs
– Brits _____	Está lleno de ingleses
	ehstah lyehnoh deh eenglehsehs

🝰 .5 Departure

See also 8.2 Settling the bill

I'm leaving tomorrow. _____ Could I settle my bill, please?	Mañana me voy. ¿Podría pagar la cuenta ahora?
	mahnyahnah meh boy. pohdreeah pahgahr lah kwehntah ahohrah?
What time should we_____ vacate?	¿A qué hora tenemos que dejar...?
	ah keh ohrah tehnehmohs keh dehhahr...?
Could I have my_____ deposit/passport back, please?	¿Me devuelve la fianza/el pasaporte?
	meh dehbwehlbeh lah fyahnthah/ehl pahsahpohrteh?
We're in a terrible hurry ___	Llevamos mucha prisa
	lyehbahmohs moochah preesah
Could you forward _____ my mail to this address?	¿Podría enviarme la correspondencia a esta dirección?
	pohdreeah ehnbyahrmeh lah kohrrehspohndehnthyah ah ehstah deerehkthyohn?
Could we leave our_____ luggage here until we leave?	¿Podríamos dejar las maletas aquí hasta que nos marchemos?
	pohdreeahmohs dehhahr lahs mahlehtahs ahkee ahstah keh nohs mahrchehmohs?
Thanks for your _____ hospitality	Muchas gracias por la hospitalidad
	moochahs grahthyahs pohr lah ohspeetahleedahdh

7 Overnight accommodation

73

Money matters

Money matters

● **In general,** banks are open to the public between 9am and 2pm; they are closed on Saturdays. In large cities it is possible to find main branches open until 4.30. To exchange currency a passport is required. Some travel agencies also provide facilities. The sign *cambio* indicates that money can be exchanged. Hotels may also offer this service, but at a less favourable rate.

8 .1 **B**anks

Where can I find a_____ bank/an exchange office around here?	¿Dónde hay un banco/una oficina de cambios por aquí? *dohndeh ay oon bahnkoh/oonah ohfeetheenah deh kahmbyohs pohr ahkee?*
Where can I cash this_____ traveller's cheque/giro cheque?	¿Dónde puedo cambiar este cheque de viajero/este cheque postal? *dohndeh pwehdoh kahmbyahr ehsteh chehkeh deh byahhehroh/ehsteh chehkeh pohstahl?*
Can I cash this...here? _____	¿Puedo cambiar aquí este...? *pwehdoh kahmbyahr ahkee ehsteh...?*
Can I withdraw money_____ on my credit card here?	¿Se puede sacar dinero con una tarjeta de crédito? *seh pwehdeh sahkahr deenehroh kohn oonah tahrhehtah deh krehdeetoh?*
What's the minimum/_____ maximum amount?	¿Cuál es el mínimo/el máximo? *kwahl ehs ehl meeneemoh/ehl mahxeemoh?*
Can I take out less_____ than that?	¿También puedo sacar menos? *tahmbyehn pwehdoh sahkahr mehnohs?*
I've had some money_____ transferred here. Has it arrived yet?	He pedido un giro telegráfico. ¿Me ha llegado ya? *eh pehdeedoh oon heeroh tehlehgrahfeekoh. meh ah lyehgahdoh yah?*
These are the details _____ of my bank in the UK	Estos son los datos de mi banco en el Reino Unido *ehstohs sohn lohs dahtohs deh mee bahnkoh ehn ehl reynoh ooneedoh*
This is my bank/giro_____ number	Este es mi número de cuenta bancaria/de la caja postal *ehsteh ehs mee noomehroh deh kwehntah bahnkahryah/deh lah kahhah pohstahl*
I'd like to change_____ some money	Quisiera cambiar dinero *keesyehrah kahmbyahr deenehroh*
– pounds into... _____	Libras esterlinas por... *leebrahs ehstehrleenahs pohr...*
– dollars into... _____	Dólares estadounidenses por... *dohlahrehs ehstahdohooneedehnsehs pohr...*
What's the exchange _____ rate?	¿A cuánto está el cambio? *ah kwahntoh ehstah ehl kahmbyoh?*
Could you give me _____ some small change with it?	¿Me podría dar sencillo/cambio? *meh pohdreeah dahr sehntheelyoh/kahmbyoh?*
This is not right _____	Esto está mal *ehstoh ehstah mahl*

Firme aquí _____	Sign here, please
Tiene que rellenar esto _____	Fill this out, please
¿Me permite su pasaporte? _____	Could I see your passport, please?
¿Me permite su carnet de identidad? ___	Could I see some identification, please?
¿Me permite su tarjeta de la _____ caja postal?	Could I see your girobank card, please?
¿Me permite su tarjeta del banco? _____	Could I see your bank card, please?

8 .2 **S**ettling the bill

Could you put it on_____ my bill?	¿Podría cargarlo a mi cuenta? *pohdreeah kahrgahrloh ah mee kwehntah?*
Does this amount _____ include service?	¿Está incluido el servicio en esta cifra? *ehstah eenklooeedoh ehl sehrbeethyoh ehn ehstah theefrah?*
Can I pay by...?_____	¿Puedo pagar con...? *pwehdoh pahgahr kohn...?*
Can I pay by credit card?___	¿Puedo pagar con tarjeta de crédito? *pwehdoh pahgahr kohn tahrhehtah deh krehdeetoh?*
Can I pay by traveller's _____ cheque?	¿Puedo pagar con un cheque de viajero? *pwehdoh pahgahr kohn oon chehkeh de byahhehroh?*
Can I pay with foreign _____ currency?	¿Puedo pagar con moneda extranjera? *pwehdoh pahgahr kohn mohnehdah ehxtrahnhehrah?*
You've given me too _____ much/you haven't given me enough change	Me ha devuelto de más/de menos *meh ah dehbwehltoh deh mahs/deh mehnohs*
Could you check the_____ bill again, please?	¿Puede volver a hacer la cuenta? *pwehdeh bohlbehr ah ahthehr lah kwehntah?*
Could I have a receipt, _____ please?	¿Podría darme un recibo? *pohdreeah dahrmeh oon rehtheeboh?*
I don't have enough _____ money on me	No me alcanza el dinero *noh meh ahlkahnthah ehl deenehroh*

No aceptamos tarjetas de _____ crédito/cheques de viajero/moneda extranjera	We don't accept credit cards/traveller's cheques/foreign currency

This is for you _____	Tenga, esto es para usted *tehngah, ehstoh ehs pahrah oostehdh*
Keep the change _____	Quédese con la vuelta *kehdehseh kohn lah bwehltah*

Post and telephone

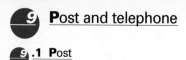

9 Post and telephone

9.1 Post

For giros, see 8 Money matters

● **Post offices** are open from Monday to Saturday from 9am to 1 or 1.30pm. However stamps (*sellos*) can be bought at any *estanco* and many hotels also provide stamps. It is advisable to post letters at a post office, rather than the yellow mail boxes (*buzón*).

giros postales money orders	telegramas telegrams	sellos stamps
paquetes parcels		

Where's...?	¿Dónde está...? *dohndeh ehstah...?*
Where's the post office?	¿Dónde hay una oficina de Correos por aquí? *dohndeh ay oonah ohfeetheenah deh kohrrehohs pohr ahkee?*
Where's the main post office?	¿Dónde está la oficina central de Correos? *dohndeh ehstah lah ohfeetheenah thehntrahl deh kohrrehohs?*
Where's the postbox?	¿Dónde hay un buzón por aquí? *dohndeh ahee oon boothohn pohr ahkee?*
Which counter should I go to...?	¿Cuál es la ventanilla para...? *kwahl ehs lah behntahneelyah pahrah...?*
– to send a fax	¿Cuál es la ventanilla para enviar un fax? *kwahl ehs lah behntahneelyah pahrah ehnbyahr oon fahx?*
– to change money	¿Cuál es la ventanilla para cambiar dinero? *kwahl ehs lah behntahneelyah pahrah kahmbyahr deenehroh?*
– to change giro cheques	¿Cuál es la ventanilla para los cheques postales? *kwahl ehs lah behntahneelyah pahrah lohs chehkehs pohstahlehs?*
– for a Telegraph Money Order?	¿Cuál es la ventanilla para los giros telegráficos? *kwahl ehs lah behntahneelyah pahrah lohs heerohs tehlehgrahfeekohs?*
Poste restante	Lista de correos *leestah deh kohrrehohs*
Is there any mail for me?My name's...	¿Hay carta para mí? Me llamo... *ay kahrtah pahrah mee? meh lyahmoh...*

Post and telephone

Stamps

What's the postage _____ for a...to...?	¿Cuánto se le pone a un(a)...para...? *kwahntoh seh leh pohneh ah oon(ah)...pahrah...?*
Are there enough _____ stamps on it?	¿Lleva suficiente franqueo? *lyehbah soofeethyehnteh frahnkehoh?*
I'd like... ...peseta stamps __	Déme...sellos de... *dehmeh...sehlyohs deh...*
I'd like to send this... _____	Quisiera enviar esto... *keesyehrah ehnbyahr ehstoh...*
– express _____	Quisiera enviar esto por correo urgente *keesyehrah ehnbyahr ehstoh pohr kohrrehoh oorhehnteh*
– by air mail _____	Quisiera enviar esto por avión *keesyehrah ehnbyahr ehstoh pohr ahbyohn*
– by registered mail _____	Quisiera enviar esto certificado *keesyehrah ehnbyahr ehstoh thehrteefeekahdoh*

Telegram / fax

I'd like to send a _____ telegram to...	Quisiera mandar un telegrama a... *keesyehrah mahndar oon tehlehgrahmah ah...*
How much is that _____ per word?	¿Cuánto cuesta por palabra? *kwahntoh kwehstah pohr pahlahbrah?*
This is the text I want _____ to send	Este es el texto que quiero enviar *ehsteh ehs ehl tehxtoh keh kyehroh ehnbyahr*
Shall I fill in the form _____ myself?	¿Relleno yo mismo el formulario? *rehlyehnoh yoh meesmoh ehl fohrmoolahryoh?*
Can I make photocopies/___ send a fax here?	¿Se pueden hacer fotocopias/se puede enviar un fax aquí? *seh pwehdehn ahthehr fohtohkohpyahs/seh pwehdeh ehnbyahr oon fahx ahkee?*
How much is it _____ per page?	¿Cuánto cuesta por página? *kwahntoh kwehstah pohr pah_hee_nah?*

9 .2 Telephone

See also 1.8 Telephone alphabet

● **All phone booths** offer a direct international service to the UK or US (07 - country code 44 (UK) or 1 (US) – trunk code minus 0 – number). Area codes are displayed. It is easier, and may even be cheaper to place your call from the *Telefónica* or telephone office. When phoning someone in Spain, you will not be greeted with the subscriber's name but *diga* or *dígame*.

Is there a phone box _____ around here?	¿Hay alguna cabina teléfonica por aquí? *ay ahlgoonah kahbeenah tehlehfohneekah pohr ahkee?*
Could I use your _____ phone, please?	¿Podría usar su teléfono? *pohdreeah oosahr soo tehlehfohnoh?*

Do you have a _____ (city/region)...phone directory?	¿Tiene una guía de teléfonos de la ciudad/la provincia de...? _tyehneh oonah gheeah deh tehlehfohnohs deh lah thyoodahdh/lah prohbeenthyah deh...?_
Where can I get a _____ phone card?	¿Dónde puedo conseguir una tarjeta de teléfonos? _dohndeh pwehdoh kohnsehgheer oonah tahr<u>h</u>ehtah deh tehlehfohnohs?_
Could you give me...? _____	¿Me podría dar...? _meh pohdreeah dahr...?_
– the number for _____ international directory enquiries	¿Me podría dar el número de información internacional? _meh pohdreeah dahr ehl noomehroh deh eenfohrmahthyohn eentehrnahthyohnahl?_
– the number of room... ___	¿Me podría dar el número de la habitación...? _meh pohdreeah dahr ehl noomehroh deh lah ahbeetahthyohn...?_
– the international _____ access code	¿Me podría dar el indicativo internacional? _meh pohdreeah dahr ehl eendeekahteeboh eentehrnahthyonahl...?_
– the country code for..._____	¿Me podría dar el indicativo de...? _meh pohdreeah dahr ehl eendeekahteeboh deh...?_
– the trunk code for... _____	¿Me podría dar el prefijo de...? _meh pohdreeah dahr ehl prehfee<u>h</u>oh deh...?_
– the number of... _____	¿Me podría dar el número de abonado de...? _meh pohdreeah dahr ehl noomehroh deh ahbohnahdoh deh...?_
Could you check if this ____ number's correct?	¿Podría controlar si está bien este número? _pohdreeah kohntrohlahr see ehstah byehn ehsteh noomehroh?_
Can I dial international_____ direct?	¿Se puede llamar directamente al extranjero? _seh pwehdeh lyahmahr deerehktahmehnteh ahl ehxtrahn<u>h</u>ehroh?_
Do I have to go through ___ the switchboard?	¿Hay que llamar por operadora? _ay keh lyahmahr pohr ohpehrahdohrah?_
Do I have to dial '0'_____ first?	¿Hay que marcar primero el cero? _ay keh mahrkahr preemehroh ehl thehroh?_
Do I have to book _____ my calls?	¿Hay que pedir línea? _ay keh pehdeer leenehah?_
Could you dial this _____ number for me, please?	¿Podría usted llamar a este número? _pohdreeah oostehdh lyahmahr ah ehsteh noomehroh?_
Could you put me _____ through to.../extension..., please?	¿Me podría poner con.../con la extensión...? _meh pohdreeah pohnehr kohn.../kohn lah ehxtehnsyohn...?_
I'd like to place a _____ reverse-charge call to...	Quisiera una llamada de cobro revertido a... _keesyehrah oonah lyahmahdah deh kohbroh rehbehrteedoh ah..._

What's the charge per ____ minute?	¿Cuánto cuesta por minuto?
	kwahntoh kwehstah pohr meenootoh?
Have there been any ____ calls for me?	¿Ha habido alguna llamada para mí?
	ah ahbeedoh ahlgoonah lyahmahdah pahrah mee?

The conversation

Hello, this is..._____	Buenos días, soy...
	bwehnohs deeahs, soy...
Who is this, please? _____	¿Con quién hablo?
	kohn kyehn ahbloh?
Is this...?_____	¿Hablo con...?
	ahbloh kohn...?
I'm sorry, I've dialled ____ the wrong number	Perdone, me he equivocado de número
	pehrdohneh, meh eh ehkeebohkahdoh deh noomehroh
I can't hear you _____	No le oigo bien
	noh leh oygoh byehn
I'd like to speak to... _____	Quisiera hablar con...
	keesyehrah ahblahr kohn...
Is there anybody _____ who speaks English?	¿Hay alguien que hable inglés?
	ay ahlghyehn keh ahbleh eenglehs?
Extension..., please_____	¿Me pone con la extensión...?
	meh pohneh kohn lah ehxtehnsyohn...?
Could you ask him/her_____ to call me back?	¿Podría decirle que me llame?
	pohdreeah dehtheerleh keh meh lyahmeh?
My name's... _____ My number's...	Me llamo...Mi número es...
	meh lyahmoh...mee noomehroh ehs...
Could you tell him/her_____ I called?	¿Puede decirle que he llamado?
	pwehdeh dehtheerleh keh eh lyahmahdoh?
I'll call back tomorrow ____	Lo/la volveré a llamar mañana
	loh/lah bohlbehreh ah lyahmahr mahnyahnah

Lo llaman por teléfono _____	There's a phone call for you
Primero tiene que marcar el cero _____	You have to dial '0' first
Un momento, por favor _____	One moment, please
No contestan _____	There's no answer
Está comunicando _____	The line's engaged
¿Quiere esperar?_____	Do you want to hold?
Ahora le paso _____	Putting you through
Se ha equivocado de número_____	You've got a wrong number
El señor/la señora...no está en estos ____ momentos.	He's/she's not here right now
El señor/la señora...no estará hasta...____	He'll/she'll be back...
Este es el contestador_____ automático de...	This is the answering machine of...

Shopping

10 **S**hopping

● **Opening times:** Monday to Friday, 9.30am-1.30pm and 5pm-8pm.
Department stores are open in the afternoons from 4pm and remain
open on Saturdays. Other shops generally close on Saturdays at 1pm.
In tourist areas shops open for longer periods.
Chemists display the list of *farmacias de guardia* (those open on
Sundays and after hours).

almacén
department store
antigüedades
antiques
artículos de deporte
sports shop
artículos del hogar
household goods
artículos dietéticos
health food shop
artículos fotográficos
camera shop
artículos usados
second hand goods
autoservicio
self service
bicicletas
bicycle shop
bodega
off licence
bricolaje
DIY-store
carnicería
butcher's shop
casa de música
music shop
centro comercial
shopping centre
comestibles
grocery store
decoración
(de interiores)
interior design shop

droguería
**household products
 and cosmetics**
electrodomésticos
electrical appliances
estanco
tobacconist
farmacia
chemist
ferretería
hardware shop
floristería
florist
frutas y verduras
greengrocer
galería comercial
shopping arcade
heladería
ice cream parlour
joyería
jeweller
juguetería
toy shop
lavandería
laundry
lechería
dairy
librería
book shop
mercado
market
mercería
draper
óptica
optician

panadería
bakery
pastelería
cake shop
peluquería (señoras,
 caballeros)
hairdresser
perfumería
cosmetics
pescadería
fishmonger
quiosco
news stand
recuerdos de viaje
souvenir shop
reparación de
 bicicletas
bicycle repair shop
revistas y prensa
newsagent
salón de belleza
beauty parlour
supermercado
supermarket
tienda
shop
tienda de modas
clothes shop
tintorería
drycleaner
zapatería
shoe shop
zapatero
cobbler

🔟 .1 Shopping conversations

Where can I get...?	¿Dónde puedo conseguir...?
	dohndeh pwehdoh kohnsehgheer...?
When does this shop open?	¿De qué hora a qué hora abren?
	deh keh ohrah ah keh ohrah ahbrehn?
Could you tell me where the...department is?	¿Me podría indicar la sección de...?
	meh pohdreeah eendeekahr lah sehkthyohn deh...?
Could you help me, please? I'm looking for...	¿Podría ayudarme? Busco...
	pohdreeah ahyoodahrmeh? booskoh...
Do you sell British/American newspapers?	¿Venden periódicos británicos/americanos?
	behndehn pehryohdeekohs breetahneekohs/ahmehreekahnohs?

🤝

¿Lo/la atienden?	**Are you being served?**

No, I'd like...	No. Quisiera...
	noh. keesyehrah...
I'm just looking, if that's all right	Sólo estoy mirando, gracias
	sohloh ehstoy meerahndoh, grahthyahs

🤝

¿Algo más?	**Anything else?**

Yes, I'd also like...	Sí, también déme...
	see, tahmbyehn dehmeh...
No, thank you. That's all	No, gracias. Es todo
	noh, grahthyahs, ehs tohdoh
Could you show me...?	¿Me podría mostrar...?
	meh pohdreeah mohstrahr...?
I'd prefer...	Prefiero...
	prehfyehroh...
This is not what I'm looking for	No es lo que busco
	noh ehs loh keh booskoh
Thank you. I'll keep looking	Gracias. Voy a seguir mirando
	grahthyahs. boy ah sehgheer meerahndoh
Do you have something...?	¿No tendría algo ...?
	noh tehndreeah ahlgoh ...?
– less expensive?	¿No tendría algo más barato?
	noh tehndreeah ahlgoh mahs bahrahtoh?
– smaller?	¿No tendría algo más pequeño?
	noh tehndreeah ahlgoh mahs pehkehnyoh?
– larger?	¿No tendría algo más grande?
	noh tehndreeah ahlgoh mahs grahndeh?
I'll take this one	Me llevo éste/ésta
	meh lyehboh ehsteh/ehstah
Does it come with instructions?	¿Viene con instrucciones?
	byehneh kohn eenstrookthyohnehs?
It's too expensive	Me parece muy caro
	meh pahrehtheh mwee kahroh

I'll give you... _____	Le doy...
	leh doy...
Could you keep this for _____ me? I'll come back for it later	¿Me lo/la podría guardar? Volveré más tarde a buscarlo
	meh loh/lah pohdreeah gwahrdahr? bohlbehreh mahs tahrdeh ah booskahrloh
Have you got a bag _____ for me, please?	¿Tendría una bolsita?
	tehndreeah oonah bohlseetah?
Could you giftwrap_____ it, please?	¿Me lo podría envolver para regalo?
	meh loh pohdreeah ehnbohlbehr pahrah rehgahloh?

10 .2 Food

I'd like a hundred_____ grams of..., please	Quisiera cien gramos de...
	keesyehrah thyehn grahmohs deh...
– half a kilo of... _____	Quisiera medio kilo de...
	keesyehrah mehdyoh keeloh deh...
– a kilo of... _____	Quisiera un kilo de...
	keesyehrah oon keeloh deh...
Could you...it for me, _____ please?	¿Me lo podría...?
	meh loh pohdreeah...?
Could you slice it/ _____ dice it for me, please?	¿Me lo podría cortar en lonchas/en trozos?
	meh loh pohdreeah kohrtahr ehn lohnchahs/ehn trohthohs?
Could you grate it _____ for me, please?	¿Me lo podría rallar?
	meh loh pohdreeah rahlyahr?
Can I order it?_____	¿Se lo podría encargar?
	seh loh pohdreeah ehnkahrgahr?
I'll pick it up tomorrow/ _____ at...	Pasaré a buscarlo mañana/a las...
	pahsahreh ah booskahrloh mahnyahnah/ah lahs...
Can you eat/drink this? _____	¿Es para comer/beber?
	ehs pahrah kohmehr/behbehr?
What's in it? _____	¿Qué lleva dentro?
	keh lyehbah dehntroh?

Shopping

10

I saw something in the ____ window. Shall I point it out?	He visto algo en el escaparate. ¿Se lo enseño? *eh beestoh ahlgoh ehn ehl ehskahpahrahteh, seh loh ehnsehnyoh?*
I'd like something to_____ go with this	Busco algo que haga juego con esto *booskoh ahlgoh keh ahgah hwehgoh kohn ehstoh*
Do you have shoes _____ in this colour?	¿Tiene zapatos de este color? *tyehneh thahpahtohs deh ehsteh kohlohr?*
I'm a size...in the UK_____	En el Reino Unido tengo el número... *ehn ehl reheenoh ooneedoh tehngoh ehl noomehroh...*
Can I try this on? _____	¿Me lo podría probar? *meh loh pohdreeah prohbahr?*
Where's the fitting_____ room?	¿Dónde está el probador? *dohndeh ehstah ehl prohbahdohr?*
It doesn't fit_____	No me vale *noh meh bahleh*
This is the right size _____	Este es mi número *ehsteh ehs mee noomehroh*
It doesn't suit me_____	No me está bien *noh meh ehstah byehn*
Do you have this/ _____ these in...?	¿Tiene éste/ésta, pero en...? *tyehneh ehsteh/ehstah pehroh ehn...?*
The heel's too high/low ___	El tacón me parece muy alto/bajo *ehl tahkohn meh pahrehtheh mwee ahltoh/bahhoh*
Is this/are these _____ genuine leather?	¿Es/son de piel auténtica? *ehs/sohn deh pyehl ah-ootehnteekah?*
I'm looking for a..._____ for a...-year-old baby/child	Busco un/una...para un bebé/niño de...años *booskoh oon/oonah...pahrah oon behbeh/neenyoh deh...ahnyohs*
I'd like a... ... _____	Quisiera un/una...de... *keesyehrah oon/oonah...deh...*
– silk _____	Quisiera un/una...de seda *keesyehrah oon/oonah...deh sehdah*
– cotton _____	Quisiera un/una...de algodón *keesyehrah oon/oonah...deh ahlgohdohn*
– woollen _____	Quisiera un/una...de lana *keesyehrah oon/oonah...deh lahnah*
– linen_____	Quisiera un/una...de hilo *keesyehrah oon/oonah...deh eeloh*
What temperature_____ can I wash it at?	¿A qué temperatura lo puedo lavar? *ah keh tehmpehrahtoorah loh pwehdoh lahbahr?*
Will it shrink in the _____ wash?	¿Encoge al lavarlo? *enkohheh ahl lahbahrloh?*

No planchar	Colgar mojado	Lavado a mano
Do not iron	**Drip dry**	**Hand wash**
No centrifugar	Lavado en seco	Lavado a máquina
Do not spin dry	**Dry clean**	**Machine wash**

At the cobbler

Could you mend _____ these shoes?	¿Podría arreglar estos zapatos?
	pohdreeah ahrrehglahr ehstohs thahpahtohs?
Could you put new _____ soles/heels on these?	¿Podría ponerle nuevas suelas/nuevos tacones?
	pohdreeah pohnehrleh nwehbahs swehlahs/nwehbohs tahkohnehs?
When will they be _____ ready?	¿Para cuándo van a estar?
	pahrah kwahndoh bahn ah ehstahr?
I'd like..., please _____	Quisiera..., por favor
	keesyehrah..., pohr fahbohr
– a tin of shoe polish _____	Quisiera una crema para zapatos
	keesyehrah oonah krehmah pahrah thahpahtohs
– a pair of shoelaces_____	Quisiera un par de cordones
	keesyehrah oon pahr deh kohrdohnehs

🔟 .4 Photographs and video

I'd like a film for this_____ camera, please	Quisiera un rollo/carrete para esta cámara
	keesyehrah oon rohlyoh/kahrrehteh pahrah ehstah kahmahrah
– a 126 cartridge _____	Quisiera una película en cassette de 126
	keesyehrah oonah pehleekoolah ehn kahseht deh thyehntoh beheenteesehees
– a 35mm colour slide _____	Un carrete de 35mm para diapositivas en color
	oon kahrrehteh deh treyntah ee theenkoh meeleemehtrohs pahrah deeapohseeteebahs ehn kohlohr
– a 35mm colour _____ print	Un carrete de 35mm en color
	oon kahrrehteh deh treyntah ee theenkoh meeleemehtrohs ehn kohlohr
– a 35mm black _____ and white	Un carrete de 35mm en blanco y negro
	oon kahrrehteh deh treyntah ee theenkoh meeleemehtrohs ehn blahnkoh ee nehgroh
– a videotape _____	Quisiera una cinta de vídeo
	keesyehrah oonah theentah deh veedehoh
colour/black and white_____	color/blanco y negro
	kohlohr/blahnkoh ee nehgroh
super eight _____	superocho
	soopehrohchoh
12/24/36 exposures _____	doce/veinticuatro/treinta y seis fotos
	dohtheh/beheenteekwahtroh/treheentah ee sehees fohtohs
ASA/DIN number_____	valor ISO
	bahlohr eesoh
daylight film _____	película para luz natural
	pehleekoolah pahrah looth nahtoorahl
film for artificial light _____	película para luz artificial
	pehleekoolah pahrah looth ahrteefeethyahl

Problems

Could you load the _____ film for me, please?	¿Me podría poner el rollo/carrete en la cámara? *meh pohdreeah pohnehr ehl rohlyoh/kahrrehteh ehn lah kahmahrah?*
Could you take the film _____ out for me, please?	¿Me podría sacar el rollo/carrete de la cámara? *meh pohdreeah sahkahr ehl rohlyoh/kahrrehteh deh lah kahmahrah?*
Should I replace _____ the batteries?	¿Tengo que cambiar las pilas? *tehngoh keh kahmbyahr lahs peelahs?*
Could you have a look _____ at my camera, please? It's not working	¿Me podría revisar la cámara? Ya no funciona *meh pohdreeah rehbeesahr lah kahmahrah? yah noh foonthyohnah*
The...is broken _____	Está estropeado el... *ehstah ehstrohpehahdoh ehl...*
The film's jammed _____	Se ha atascado el rollo/carrete *seh ah ahtahskahdoh ehl rohlyoh /kahrrehteh*
The film's broken _____	Se ha roto el rollo/carrete *seh ah rohtoh ehl rohlyoh/kahrrehteh*
The flash isn't working ____	No funciona el flash *noh foonthyohnah ehl flahsh*

Processing and prints

I'd like to have this film ____ developed/printed, please	Quisiera mandar a revelar/copiar este rollo/carrete *keesyehrah mahndahr ah rehbehlahr/kohpyahr ehsteh rohlyoh/kahrrehteh*
I'd like...prints from _____ each negative	Quisiera...copias de cada negativo *keesyehrah...kohpyahs deh kahdah nehgahteeboh*
glossy/mat _____	brillante/mate *breelyahnte/mahteh*
I'd like to reorder _____ these photos	Quisiera encargar más copias de estas fotos *keesyehrah ehnkahrgahr mahs kohpyahs deh ehstahs fohtohs*
I'd like to have this _____ photo enlarged	Quisiera una ampliación de esta foto *keesyehrah oonah ahmplyahthyohn deh ehstah fohtoh*
How much is _____ processing?	¿Cuánto sale el revelado? *kwahntoh sahleh ehl rehbehlahdoh?*
– printing? _____	¿Cuánto sale el copiado? *kwahntoh sahleh ehl kohpyahdoh?*
– extra copies? _____	¿Cuánto salen las copias adicionales? *kwahntoh sahlehn lahs kohpyahs ahdeethyohnahlehs?*
– the enlargement? _____	¿Cuánto sale la ampliación? *kwahntoh sahleh lah ahmplyahthyohn?*
When will they _____ be ready?	¿Para cuándo van a estar? *pahrah kwahndoh bahn ah ehstahr?*

Do I have to make an _____ appointment?	¿Tengo que pedir hora? *tehngoh keh pehdeer ohrah?*
Can I come in straight _____ away?	¿Podría atenderme en seguida? *pohdreeah ahtehndehrmeh ehn sehgheedah?*
How long will I have_____ to wait?	¿Cuánto tengo que esperar? *kwahntoh tehngoh keh ehspehrahr?*
I'd like a shampoo/ _____ haircut	Quisiera lavarme/cortarme el pelo *keesyehrah lahbahrmeh/kohrtahrmeh ehl pehloh*
I'd like a shampoo for _____ oily/dry hair, please	Quisiera un champú para cabello graso/seco *keesyehrah oon chahmpoo pahrah kahbehlyoh grahsoh/sehkoh*
an anti-dandruff_____ shampoo	Quisiera un champú anticaspa *keesyehrah oon chahmpoo ahnteekahspah*
– a shampoo for_____ permed/coloured hair	Quisiera un champú para cabello con permanente/teñido. *keesyehrah oon chahmpoo pahrah kahbehlyoh kohn pehrmahnehnteh/tehnyeedoh*
– a colour rinse shampoo __	Quisiera un champú color *keesyehrah oon chahmpoo kohlohr*
– a shampoo with _____ conditioner	Quisiera un champú con acondicionador *keesyehrah oon chahmpoo kohn ahkohndeethyohnahdohr*
– highlights _____	Quisiera que me hagan claritos *keesyehrah keh meh ahgahn klahreetohs*
Do you have a colour_____ chart, please?	¿Tendría una carta de colores? *tehndreeah oonah kahrtah deh kohlohrehs?*
I want to keep it the _____ same colour	Quiero conservar el mismo color *kyehroh kohnsehrbahr ehl meesmoh kohlohr*
I'd like it darker/lighter _____	Quisiera un color más oscuro/más claro *keesyehrah oon kohlohr mahs ohskooroh/mahs klahroh*
I'd like/I don't want _____ hairspray	(No) quiero fijador *(noh) kyehroh feehahdohr*
– gel_____	(No) quiero gel *(noh) kyehroh hehl*
– lotion _____	(No) quiero loción *(noh) kyehroh lohthyohn*
I'd like a short fringe _____	Quisiera el flequillo corto *keesyehrah ehl flehkeelyoh kohrtoh*
Not too short at _____ the back	No lo quisiera demasiado corto por detrás *noh loh keesyehrah dehmahsyahdoh kohrtoh pohr dehtrahs*
Not too long here _____	No lo quisiera demasiado largo aquí *noh loh keesyehrah dehmahsyahdoh lahrgoh ahkee*
I'd like/I don't want _____ (many) curls	(No) quisiera (demasiados) rizos *(noh) keesyehrah (dehmahsyadohs) reethohs*

English	Spanish
It needs a little/___ a lot taken off	Hay que cortar sólo un trocito/un buen trozo *ay keh kohrtahr sohloh oon trohtheetoh/oon bwehn trohthoh*
I want a completely ___ different style	Quisiera un modelo totalmente diferente *keesyehrah oon mohdehloh tohtahlmehnteh deefehrehnteh*
I'd like it the same as... ___	Quisiera el pelo como... *keesyehrah ehl pehloh kohmoh...*
– as that lady's ___	Quisiera el pelo como esa señora *keesyehrah ehl pehloh kohmoh ehsah sehnyohrah*
– as in this photo___	Quisiera el pelo como en esta foto *keesyehrah ehl pehloh kohmoh ehn ehstah fohtoh*
Could you put the ___ drier up/down a bit?	¿Podría poner el casco más alto/bajo? *pohdreeah pohnehr ehl kahskoh mahs ahltoh/mahs bahhoh?*
I'd like a facial___	Quisiera una máscara facial *keesyehrah oonah mahskahrah fahthyahl*
– a manicure ___	Quisiera que me hagan manicura *keesyehrah keh meh ahgahn mahneekoorah*
– a massage ___	Quisiera que me hagan masaje *keesyehrah keh meh ahgahn mahsahheh*
Could you trim ___ my fringe?	¿Me podría recortar el flequillo? *meh pohdreeah rehkohrtahr ehl flehkeelyoh?*
– my beard? ___	¿Me podría recortar la barba? *meh pohdreeah rehkohrtahr lah bahrbah?*
– my moustache? ___	¿Me podría recortar el bigote? *meh pohdreeah rehkohrtahr ehl beegohteh?*
I'd like a shave, please___	Aféiteme, por favor *ahfeheetehmeh, pohr fahbohr*
I'd like a wet shave, ___	Aféiteme a navaja, por favor

Spanish	English
¿Cómo quiere el corte de pelo? ___	How do you want it cut?
¿Qué modelo deseaba? ___	What style did you have in mind?
¿Qué color quiere?___	What colour do you want it?
¿Esta temperatura le va bien?___	Is the temperature all right for you?
¿Quiere algo para leer?___	Would you like something to read?
¿Quiere algo para beber?___	Would you like a drink?
¿Así está bien? ___	Is this what you had in mind?

please	*ahfeheetehmeh ah nahbahhhah, pohr fahbohr*

At the Tourist Information Centre

11 .1 Places of interest

Where's the Tourist Information, please?	¿Dónde está la oficina de turismo?
	dohndeh ehstah lah ohfeetheenah deh tooreesmoh?
Do you have a city map?	¿Tendría un plano de la ciudad?
	tehndreeah oon plahnoh deh lah thyoodahdh?
Where is the museum?	¿Dónde está el museo?
	dohndeh ehstah ehl moosehoh?
Where can I find a church?	¿Dónde podría encontrar una iglesia?
	dohndeh pohdreeah ehnkohntrahr oonah eeglehsyah?
Could you give me some information about...?	¿Me podría dar información sobre...?
	meh pohdreeah dahr eenfohrmahthyohn sohbreh...?
How much is that?	¿Cuánto le debemos por esto?
	kwahntoh leh dehbehmohs pohr ehstoh?
What are the main places of interest?	¿Cuáles son los sitios más interesantes para visitar?
	kwahlehs sohn lohs seetyohs mahs eentehrehsahntehs pahrah veeseetahr?
Could you point them out on the map?	¿Me los podría señalar en el plano?
	meh lohs pohdreeah sehnyahlahr ehn ehl plahnoh?
What do you recommend?	¿Qué nos recomienda?
	keh nohs rehkohmyehndah?
We'll be here for a few hours	Pensamos quedarnos unas horas
	pehnsahmohs kehdahrnohs oonahs ohrahs
– a day	Pensamos quedarnos un día
	pehnsahmohs kehdahrnohs oon deeah
– a week	Pensamos quedarnos una semana
	pehnsahmohs kehdahrnohs oonah sehmahnah
We're interested in...	Nos interesa...
	nohs eentehrehsah...
Is there a scenic walk around the city?	¿Hay algún circuito turístico para visitar la ciudad a pie?
	ay ahlgoon theerkweetoh tooreesteekoh pahrah veeseetar lah thyoodahdh ah pyeh?
How long does it take?	¿Cuánto dura?
	kwahntoh doorah?
Where does it start/end?	¿De dónde sale?/¿Dónde termina?
	deh dohndeh sahleh?/dohndeh tehrmeenah?
Are there any boat cruises here?	¿Hay excursiones en barco?
	ay ehxkoorsyohnehs ehn bahrkoh?
Where can we board?	¿Dónde se puede embarcar?
	dohndeh seh pwehdeh ehmbahrkahr?
Are there any bus tours?	¿Hay excursiones en autocar?
	ay ehxkoorsyohnehs ehn ahootohkahr?
Where do we get on?	¿De dónde salen?
	deh dohndeh sahlehn?
Is there a guide who speaks English?	¿Hay algún guía que hable inglés?
	ay ahlgoon gheeah keh ahbleh eenglehs?

What trips can we take around the area?	¿Qué excursiones se pueden hacer en los alrededores? *keh ehxkoorsyohnehs seh pwehdehn ahthehr ehn lohs ahlrehdehdohrehs?*
Are there any _____ excursions?	¿Hay excursiones organizadas? *ay ehxkoorsyohnehs ohrgahneethahdahs?*
Where do they go to? _____	¿Hacia dónde van? *ahthyah dohndeh bahn?*
We'd like to go to..._____	Quisiéramos ir a... *keesyehrahmohs eer ah...*
How long is the trip? _____	¿Cuánto se tarda en llegar? *kwahntoh seh tahrdah ehn lyehgahr?*
How long do we _____ stay in...?	¿Cuánto dura la visita a...? *kwahntoh doorah lah beeseetah ah...*
Are there any guided _____ tours?	¿Hay visitas guiadas? *ay beeseetahs gheeahdahs?*
How much free time_____ will we have there?	¿Cuánto tiempo libre tenemos allí? *kwahntoh tyehmpoh leebreh tehnehmohs alyee?*
We want to go hiking _____	Nos gustaría hacer una excursión a pie *nohs goostahreeah ahthehr oonah ehxkoorsyohn ah pyeh*
Can we hire a guide? _____	¿Es posible contratar un guía? *ehs pohseebleh kohntrahtahr oon gheeah?*
Can I book mountain _____ huts?	¿Se puede hacer una reserva para un refugio (en la montaña)? *seh pwehdeh ahthehr oonah rehsehrbah pahrah oon rehfoohyoh (ehn lah mohntahnyah)?*
What time does... _____ open/close?	¿A qué hora abre/cierra...? *ah keh ohrah ahbreh/thyehrrah...?*
What days is...open/_____ closed?	¿Qué días tiene abierto/cerrado...? *keh deeahs tyehneh ahbyehrtoh/thehrrahdoh...?*
What's the admission_____ price?	¿Cuánto sale la entrada? *kwahntoh sahleh lah ehntrahdah?*
Is there a group _____ discount?	¿Hay descuento para grupos? *ay dehskwehntoh pahrah groopohs?*
Is there a child _____ discount?	¿Hay descuento para niños? *ay dehskwehntoh pahrah neenyohs?*
Is there a discount_____ for pensioners?	¿Hay descuento para jubilados? *ay dehskwehntoh pahrah hoobeelahdohs?*
Can I take (flash) _____ photos/can I film here?	¿Se pueden sacar fotos (con flash)/filmar aquí? *seh pwehdehn sahkahr fohtohs(kohn flahsh)/feelmahr ahkee?*
Do you have any _____ postcards of...?	¿Venden postales de...? *behndehn pohstahlehs deh...?*
Do you have an _____ English...?	¿Tiene un...en inglés? *tyehneh oon...ehn eenglehs?*
– an English catalogue?_____	¿Tiene un catálogo en inglés? *tyehneh oon kahtahlohgoh ehn eenglehs?*
– an English programme?_____	¿Tiene un programa en inglés? *tyehneh oon prohgrahmah ehn eenglehs?*
– an English brochure? _____	¿Tiene un folleto en inglés? *tyehneh oon fohlyehtoh ehn eenglehs?*

11 .2 Going out

● **At the cinema** most films are dubbed in Spanish. Sometimes there are only two showings, in the evening, at 7 and 11pm. In this case advance booking is advisable.

Do you have this _____ week's/month's entertainment guide?	¿Tiene la guía de los espectáculos de esta semana/este mes? *tyehneh lah gheeah deh lohs ehspehktahkoolohs deh ehstah sehmahnah/ehsteh mehs?*
What's on tonight? _____	¿Adónde podríamos ir esta noche? *ahdohndeh pohdreeahmohs eer ehstah nohcheh?*
We want to go to... _____	Nos gustaría ir a... *nohs goostahreeah eer ah...*
Which films are _____ showing?	¿Qué películas dan? *keh pehleekoolahs dahn?*
What sort of film is that?___	¿Qué clase de película es? *keh klahseh deh pehleekoolah ehs?*
suitable for everyone _____	para todos los públicos *pahrah tohdohs lohs poobleekohs*
not suitable for_____ children	prohibido para menores de 12/16 años *proheebeedoh pahrah mehnohrehs deh dohtheh/dyehtheesehees ahnyohs*
original version _____	versión original *behrsyohn ohree<u>h</u>eenahl*
subtitled _____	subtitulada *soobteetoolahdah*
dubbed _____	doblada *dohblahdah*
Is it a continuous_____ showing?	¿Es sesión continua? *ehs sehsyohn kohnteenooah?*
What's on at...? _____	¿Qué dan en...? *keh dahn ehn...?*
– the theatre? _____	¿Qué dan en el teatro? *keh dahn ehn ehl tehahtroh?*
– the concert hall?_____	¿Qué dan en la sala de conciertos? *keh dahn ehn lah sahlah deh kohnthyehrtohs?*
– the opera? _____	¿Qué dan en la ópera? *keh dahn ehn lah ohpehrah?*
Where can I find a good ___ disco around here?	¿Dónde hay una buena discoteca por aquí? *dohndeh ay oonah bwehnah deeskohtehkah pohr ahkee?*
Is it for members only? ____	¿Hay que ser socio? *ay keh sehr sohthyoh?*
Where can I find a good ___ cabaret club around here?	¿Dónde hay un buen cabaret por aquí? *dohndeh ay oon bwehn kahbahreh pohr ahkee?*
Is it evening wear only? ___	¿Hay que ir en traje de etiqueta? *ay keh eer ehn trah<u>h</u>eh deh ehteekehtah?*

Should I/we dress up? _____	¿Es recomendable ir en traje de etiqueta? *ehs rehkohmehndahbleh eer ehn trahhheh deh ehteekehtah?*
What time does the _____ show start?	¿A qué hora comienza el espectáculo? *ah keh ohrah ehmpyehthah ehl ehspehktahkooloh?*
When's the next soccer _____ match?	¿Cuándo es el próximo partido de fútbol? *kwahlndoh ehs ehl prohxeemoh pahrteedoh deh footbohl?*
Who's playing?_____	¿Quiénes juegan? *kyehnehs hwehgahn?*
I'd like an escort for tonight. Could you arrange that for me?	Quisiera contratar un/una acompañante para esta noche. ¿Podría hacerme una reserva? *keesyehrah kohntrahtahr oon/oonah ahkohmpahnyahnteh pahrah ehstah nohcheh. podreeah ahthehrmeh oonah rehsehrbah?*

11 .3 Booking tickets

Could you book some _____ tickets for us?	¿Podría hacernos una reserva? *pohdreeah ahthehrnohs oonah rehsehrbah?*
We'd like to book... _____ tickets/a table...	Quisiéramos...entradas/una mesa... *keesyehrahmohs...ehntrahdahs/oonah mehsah...*
– tickets/seats in the _____ stalls	Quisiéramos...entradas en la platea *keesyehrahmohs...ehntrahdahs ehn lah plahtehah*
– tickets/seats on the _____ balcony	Quisiéramos...entradas en el palco *keesyehrahmohs...ehntrahdahs ehn ehl pahlkoh*
– box seats _____	Quisiéramos...entradas en el palco privado *keesyehrahmohs...ehntrahdahs ehn ehl pahlkoh preebahdoh*
– a table at the front _____	Quisiéramos una mesa adelante *keesyehrahmohs oonah mehsah ahdehlahnteh*
– in the middle _____	Quisiéramos una mesa al centro *keesyehrahmohs oonah mehsah ahl thehntroh*
– at the back _____	Quisiéramos una mesa atrás *keesyehrahmohs oonah mehsah ahtrahs*
Could I book...seats for the...o'clock performance?	¿Podría reservar...entradas para la función de las...? *pohdreeah rehsehrbahr...ehntrahdahs pahrah lah foonthyohn deh lahs...?*
Are there any seats left _____ for tonight?	¿Quedan entradas para esta noche? *kehdahn ehntrahdahs pahrah ehstah nohcheh?*
How much is a ticket? _____	¿Cuánto sale la entrada? *kwahntoh sahleh lah ehntrahdah?*

When can I pick the _____ tickets up?	¿Cuándo puedo pasar a retirar las entradas?
	kwahndoh pwehdoh pahsahr ah rehteerahr lahs ehntrahdahs?
I've got a reservation _____	Tengo una reserva
	tehngoh oonah rehsehrbah
My name's... _____	Me llamo...
	meh lyahmoh...

¿Para qué función desea reservar? _____	Which performance do you want to book for?
¿Qué sector prefiere? _____	Where would you like to sit?
No hay billetes. _____	Everything's sold out
Sólo quedan entradas de pie _____	It's standing room only
Sólo quedan entradas en el palco _____	We've only got balcony seats left
Sólo quedan entradas en la galería _____	We've only got seats left in the gallery
Sólo quedan entradas en la platea _____	We've only got stalls seats left
Sólo quedan entradas adelante _____	We've only got seats left at the front
Sólo quedan entradas atrás _____	We've only got seats left at the back
¿Cuántas entradas quiere? _____	How many seats would you like?
Tiene que retirar las entradas antes de las... _____	You'll have to pick up the tickets before...o'clock
¿Me permite las entradas? _____	Tickets, please
Este es su asiento _____	This is your seat

Sports

12 Sports

12.1 Sporting questions

Where can we... around here?	¿Dónde se puede...?
	dohndeh seh pwehdeh...?
Is there a... around here?	¿Hay algún...por aquí cerca?
	ahee ahlgoon...pohr ahkee thehrkah?
Can I hire a...here?	¿Alquilan...?
	ahlkeelahn...?
Can I take...lessons?	¿Dan clases de...?
	dahn klahsehs deh...?
How much is that per hour/per day/class?	¿Cuánto sale por hora/día/clase?
	kwahntoh sahleh pohr ohrah/deeah/klahseh?
Do I need a permit for that?	¿Se necesita un permiso?
	seh nehthehseetah oon pehrmeesoh?
Where can I get the permit?	¿Dónde se consiguen los permisos?
	dohndeh seh kohnseeghehn lohs pehrmeesohs?

12.2 By the waterfront

Is it a long way to the sea still?	¿Falta mucho para llegar al mar?
	fahltah moochoh pahrah lyehgahr ahl mahr?
Is there a...around here?	¿Hay algún...por aquí?
	ay ahlgoon...pohr ahkee?
– an outdoor/indoor/ public swimming pool	¿Hay alguna piscina por aquí?
	ay ahlgoonah peestheenah pohr ahkee?
– a sandy beach	¿Hay alguna playa con arena por aquí?
	ay ahlgoonah plahyah kohn ahrehnah pohr ahkee?
– a nudist beach	¿Hay alguna playa nudista por aquí?
	ay ahlgoonah plahya noodeestah pohr ahkee?
– mooring	¿Hay algún atracadero por aquí?
	ay ahlgoon ahtrahkahdehroh pohr ahkee?
Are there any rocks here?	¿Hay rocas?
	ay rohkahs?
When's high/low tide?	¿Cuándo sube/baja la marea?
	kwahndoh soobeh/bah__hah__ lah mahrehah?
What's the water temperature?	¿Qué temperatura tiene el agua?
	keh tehmpehrahtoorah tyehneh ehl ahgwah?
Is it (very) deep here?	¿Es (muy) profundo?
	ehs mwee prohfoondoh?
Can you stand here?	¿Se puede hacer pie?
	seh pwehdeh ahtehr pyeh?
Is it safe to swim here?	¿Es seguro para nadar?
	ehs sehgooroh pahrah nahdahr?
Are there any currents?	¿Hay corriente?
	ay kohrryehnteh?
Are there any rapids/ waterfalls in this river?	¿Este río tiene rápidos/cascadas?
	ehsteh reeoh tyehneh rahpeedohs/kahskahdahs?
What does that flag/ buoy mean?	¿Qué significa aquella bandera/boya?
	keh seegneefeekah ahkehlyah bahndehrah/bohyah?

Sports

12

English	Spanish	Pronunciation
Is there a life guard on duty here?	¿Hay algún vigilante de servicio?	*ay ahlgoon veeheelante deh sehrbeetheeoh?*
Are dogs allowed here?	¿Está permitido traer perros?	*ehstah pehrmeeteedoh trahehr pehrrohs?*
Is camping on the beach allowed?	¿Está permitido acampar en la playa?	*ehstah pehrmeeteedoh ahkahmpahr ehn lah plahyah?*
Are we allowed to build a fire here?	¿Está permitido hacer fuego?	*ehstah pehrmeeteedoh ahthehr fwehgoh?*

Peligro	Prohibido pescar	Prohibido bañarse
Danger	No fishing	No swimming
Aguas de pesca	Prohibido hacer	Permiso obligatorio
Fishing water	surfing	Permits only
	No surfing	

🔢 .3 In the snow

English	Spanish	Pronunciation
Can I take ski lessons here?	¿Dan clases de esquí?	*dahn klahsehs deh eskee?*
for beginners/advanced	para principiantes/avanzados	*pahrah preentheepyahntehs/ahbahnthahdohs*
How large are the groups?	¿De cuántas personas son los grupos?	*deh kwahntahs pehrsohnahs sohn lohs groopohs?*
What language are the classes in?	¿En qué idioma son las clases?	*ehn keh eedyohmah sohn lahs klahsehs?*
I'd like a lift pass, please	Quisiera un pase para las telesillas	*keesyehrah oon pahseh pahrah lahs tehlehseelyahs*
Must I give you a passport photo?	¿Se necesita foto?	*seh nehthehseetah fohtoh?*
Where can I have a passport photo taken?	¿Dónde puedo sacarme fotos?	*dohndeh pwehdoh sahkahrmeh fohtohs?*
Where are the beginners' slopes?	¿Dónde están las pistas para principiantes?	*dohndeh ehstahn lahs peestahs pahrah preentheepyahntehs?*
Are there any runs for cross-country skiing?	¿Hay pistas de esquí de fondo por aquí?	*ay peestahs deh ehskee deh fohndoh pohr ahkee?*
Have the cross-country runs been marked?	¿Las pistas de esquí de fondo están señalizadas?	*lahs peestahs deh ehskee deh fohndoh ehstahn sehnyahleethahdahs?*
Are the...in operation?	¿Están abiertos los...?	*ehstahn ahbyehrtohs lohs...?*
– the ski lifts	¿Ya funcionan los telesquís?	*yah foonthyohnahn lohs tehlehskees?*
– the chair lifts	¿Ya funcionan las telesillas?	*yah foonthyohnahn lahs tehlehseelyahs?*
Are the slopes usable?	¿Están abiertas las pistas?	*ehstahn ahbyehrtahs lahs peestahs?*

Sports

12

Sickness

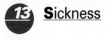

13 **S**ickness

13 .1 **C**all (fetch) the doctor

Could you call/fetch a_____ doctor quickly, please?	¿Podría llamar/ir a buscar rápido a un médico, por favor? *pohdreeah lyahmahr/eer ah booskahr rahpeedoh ah oon mehdeekoh, pohr fahbohr?*
When does the doctor ____ have surgery?	¿Cuándo tiene consulta el médico? *kwahndoh tyeneh kohnsooltah ehl mehdeekoh?*
When can the doctor ____ come?	¿Cuándo puede venir el médico? *kwahndoh pwehdeh behneer ehl mehdeekoh?*
I'd like to make an_____ appointment to see the doctor	¿Podría pedirme hora con el médico? *pohdreeah pehdeermeh ohrah kohn ehl mehdeekoh?*
I've got an appointment ___ to see the doctor at...	Tengo hora con el médico para las... *tehngoh ohrah kohn ehl mehdeekoh pahrah lahs...*
Which doctor/chemist _____ has night/weekend duty?	¿Qué médico/farmacia está de guardia esta noche/este fin de semana? *keh mehdeekoh/fahrmahthyah ehstah deh gwahrdyah ehstah nohcheh/ehsteh feen deh sehmahnah?*

13 .2 **P**atient's ailments

I don't feel well _____	No me siento bien *noh meh syehntoh byehn*
I'm dizzy_____	Tengo mareos *tehngoh mahrehohs*
– ill_____	Estoy enfermo *ehstoy ehnfehrmoh*
– sick _____	Tengo náuseas *tehngoh nahoosehahs*
I've got a cold_____	Estoy acatarrado *ehstoy ahkahtahrrahdoh*
It hurts here _____	Me duele aquí *meh dwehleh ahkee*
I've been throwing up ____	He devuelto *eh dehbwehltoh*
I've got... _____	Tengo molestias de... *tehngoh mohlehstyahs deh...*
I'm running a _____ temperature of...degrees	Tengo...grados de fiebre *tehngoh...grahdohs deh fyehbreh*
I've been stung by_____ a wasp	Me ha picado una avispa *meh ah peekahdoh oonah ahbeespah*
I've been stung by an_____ insect	Me ha picado un insecto *meh ah peekahdoh oon eensehktoh*
I've been bitten by _____ a dog	Me ha mordido un perro *meh ah mohrdeedoh oon pehrroh*
I've been stung by_____ a jellyfish	Me ha picado una medusa *meh ah peekahdoh oonah mehdoosah*

Sickness

13

I've been bitten by _____ | Me ha mordido una serpiente
a snake | *meh ah mohrdeedoh oonah sehrpyehnteh*
I've been bitten by _____ | Me ha picado un insecto
an animal | *meh ah peekahdoh oon eensehktoh*
I've cut myself _____ | Me he cortado
| *meh eh kohrtahdoh*
I've burned myself _____ | Me he quemado
| *meh eh kehmahdoh*
I've grazed myself_____ | Tengo una rozadura
| *tehngoh oonah rohthahdoorah*
I've had a fall _____ | Me he caído
| *meh eh kaheedoh*
I've sprained my ankle_____ | Me he torcido el tobillo
| *meh eh tohrtheedoh ehl tohbeelyoh*
I've come for the _____ | Vengo a que me dé una píldora del día
morning-after pill | después
| *behngoh ah keh meh deh oonah peeldohrah*
| *dehl deeah dehspwehs*

🖐 .3 The consultation

¿Qué molestias tiene? _____ | What seems to be the
| problem?
¿Cuánto hace que tiene estas _____ | How long have you had
molestias? | these symptoms?
¿Ha tenido estas molestias _____ | Have you had this trouble
anteriormente? | before?
¿Qué temperatura tiene? _____ | How high is your
| temperature?
Desnúdese._____ | Get undressed, please
Desvístase de la cintura para arriba _____ | Strip to the waist, please
Allí puede quitarse la ropa_____ | You can undress there
Descúbrase el brazo_____ | Roll up your left/right
izquierdo/derecho | sleeve, please
Recuéstese aquí _____ | Lie down here, please
¿Le duele esto? _____ | Does this hurt?
Respire hondo _____ | Breathe deeply
Abra la boca_____ | Open your mouth

Patient's medical history

I'm a diabetic _____ | Soy diabético
| *soy deeahbehteekoh*
I have a heart condition_____ | Soy enfermo cardíaco
| *soy ehnfehrmoh kahrdeeahkoh*
I have asthma_____ | Soy asmático
| *soy ahsmahteekoh*
I'm allergic to... _____ | Soy alérgico a...
| *soy ahlehrheekoh ah...*
I'm...months pregnant _____ | Estoy embarazada de...meses
| *ehstoy ehmbahrahthadah deh...mehsehs*
I'm on a diet _____ | Sigo una dieta
| *seegoh oonah dyehtah*

I'm on medication/ _____ the pill	Tomo medicamentos/la píldora
	tohmoh mehdeekahmehntohs/lah peeldohrah
I've had a heart attack _____ once before	He tenido un ataque cardíaco anteriormente
	eh tehneedoh oon ahtahkeh kahrdeeahkoh ahntehryohrmehnteh
I've had a(n)...operation ___	Me han operado del/de la...
	meh ahn ohpehrahdoh dehl/deh lah...
I've been ill recently _____	He estado enfermo hace poco
	eh ehstahdoh ehnfehrmoh ahtheh pohkoh
I've got an ulcer_____	Tengo una úlcera
	tehngoh oonah oolthehrah
I've got my period_____	Tengo la regla
	tehngoh lah rehglah

¿Padece alguna alergia?_____	Do you have any allergies?
¿Toma medicamentos?_____	Are you on any medication?
¿Sigue alguna dieta?_____	Are you on a diet?
¿Está embarazada?_____	Are you pregnant?
¿Está vacunado/a contra el tétanos?_____	Have you had a tetanus injection?

No es nada grave_____	It's nothing serious
Se ha fracturado el/la..._____	Your...is broken
Se ha contusionado el/la..._____	You've got a/some bruised...
Se ha desgarrado el/la..._____	You've got (a) torn...
Tiene una inflamación_____	You've got an inflammation
Tiene apendicitis_____	You've got appendicitis
Tiene bronquitis _____	You've got bronchitis
Tiene una enfermedad venérea _____	You've got a venereal disease
Tiene gripe _____	You've got the flu
Ha tenido un ataque al corazón _____	You've had a heart attack
Tiene una infección virósica/ bacteriana _____	You've got an infection (viral..., bacterial...)
Tiene una pulmonía_____	You've got pneumonia
Tiene una úlcera_____	You've got an ulcer
Se ha distendido un músculo _____	You've pulled a muscle
Tiene una infección vaginal_____	You've got a vaginal infection
Tiene una intoxicación alimenticia _____	You've got food poisoning

Sickness

13

Tiene una insolación _____	You've got sunstroke
Es alérgico a... _____	You're allergic to...
Está embarazada _____	You're pregnant
Quisiera hacerle un análisis de sangre/de orina/de materia fecal	I'd like to have your blood/urine/stools tested
Hay que suturar la herida _____	It needs stitching
Lo/la voy a derivar a un especialista/a ___ un hospital	I'm referring you to a specialist/sending you to hospital
Tiene que hacerse radiografías _____	You'll need to have some x-rays taken
Vuelva a tomar asiento en la sala de ___ espera	Could you wait in the waiting room, please?
Hay que operarlo/operarla _____	You'll need an operation

The diagnosis

Is it contagious? _____	¿Es contagioso?
	ehs kohntah<u>h</u>yohsoh?
How long do I have to ___ stay...?	¿Hasta cuándo tengo que...?
	ahstah kwahndoh tehngoh keh...?
– in bed _____	¿Hasta cuándo tengo que guardar cama?
	ahstah kwahndoh tehngoh keh gwahrdahr kahmah?
– in hospital _____	¿Hasta cuándo tengo que quedarme en el hospital?
	ahstah kwahndoh tehngoh keh kehdahrmeh ehn ehl ohspeetahl?
Do I have to go on ___ a special diet?	¿Tengo que seguir alguna dieta?
	tehngoh keh sehgheer ahlgoonah dyehtah?
Am I allowed to travel? ___	¿Puedo viajar?
	pwehdoh byah<u>h</u>ahr?
Can I make a new _____ appointment?	¿Puedo volver a pedir hora?
	pwehdoh bohlbehr ah pehdeer ohrah?
When do I have to _____ come back?	¿Cuándo tengo que volver?
	kwahndoh tehngoh keh bohlbehr?
I'll come back _____ tomorrow	Vuelvo mañana
	bwehlboh mahnyahnah

Vuelva mañana/dentro de...días _____	Come back tomorrow/in...days' time

13.4 Medication and prescriptions

How do I take this _____ medicine?	¿Cómo se toman estos medicamentos?
	kohmoh seh tohmahn ehstohs mehdeekahmehntohs?
How many capsules/ _____ drops/injections/ spoonfuls/tablets each time?	¿Cuántas cápsulas/gotas/inyecciones/ cucharadas/tabletas por vez?
	kwahntahs kahpsoolahs/gohtahs/eenyehkthyohnehs/koo chahrahdahs pohr behth?

How many times a day? ___	¿Cuántas veces al día?
	kwahntahs behthehs ahl deeah?
I've forgotten my_____ medication. At home I take...	Se me ha olvidado traer los medicamentos. En casa tomo...
	seh meh ah olbeedahdoh trahehr lohs mehdeekahmehntohs. ehn kahsah tohmoh...
Could you make out a ____ prescription for me?	¿Podría hacerme una receta?
	pohdreeah ahtehrmeh oonah rehthehtah?

Voy a recetarle unos antibióticos/un____ jarabe/un calmante/ unos analgésicos — I'm prescribing antibiotics/a mixture/a tranquillizer/pain killers

Tiene que guardar reposo _____ Have lots of rest

No tiene que salir a la calle _____ Stay indoors

Tiene que guardar cama_____ Stay in bed

---

antes de cada comida	inyecciones	tragar entero
before meals	injections	swallow whole
cápsulas	para uso externo	tabletas
capsules	exclusivamente	tablets
diluir en agua	not for internal use	tomar/ingerir
dissolve in water	ungüento	take
gotas	ointment	estos medicamentos
drops	aplicar/embadurnar	afectan la capacidad
cada...horas	rub on	de conducir
every...hours	cucharadas (soperas/	this medication
seguir la cura hasta	cucharaditas)	impairs your driving
el final	spoonfuls	...vez/veces cada 24
finish the course	(tablespoons/	horas
durante...días	tea-spoons)	...times a day
for...days		

13.5 At the dentist's

Do you know a good _____ dentist?	¿Me podría recomendar un buen dentista?
	meh pohdreeah rehkohmehndahr oon bwehn dehnteestah?
Could you make a _____ dentist's appointment for me? It's urgent	¿Me podría pedir hora con el dentista? Es urgente
	meh pohdreeah pehdeer ohrah kohn ehl dehnteestah? ehs oorhehnteh
Can I come in today,_____ please?	¿Me podría atender hoy mismo?
	meh pohdreeah ahtehndehr oy meesmoh?
I have (terrible)_____ toothache	Tengo (un terrible) dolor de muelas
	tehngoh (oon tehrreebleh) dohlohr deh mwehlahs
Could you prescribe/ _____ give me a painkiller?	¿Me podría recetar/dar un analgésico?
	meh pohdreeah rehthehtahr/dahr oon ahnahlhehseekoh?

English	Spanish
A piece of my tooth has broken off	Se me ha caído un pedazo de un diente *seh meh ah kaheedoh oon pehdahthoh deh oon dyehnteh*
My filling's come out	Se me ha salido un empaste *seh meh ah sahleedoh oon ehmpahsteh*
I've got a broken crown	Se me ha roto la corona *seh meh ah rohtoh lah kohrohnah*
I'd like/I don't want a local anaesthetic	Quisiera que/no quiero que me ponga anestesia local *keesyehrah keh/noh kyehroh keh meh pohngah ahnehstehsyah lohkahl*
Can you do a makeshift repair job?	¿Me podría hacer un arreglo provisional? *meh pohdreeah ahthehr oon ahrrehgloh prohbeesyohnahl?*
I don't want this tooth pulled	No quiero que me extraiga esta muela *noh kyehroh keh meh ehxtraheegah ehstah mwehlah*
My dentures are broken. Can you fix them?	Se me ha roto la dentadura postiza ¿Podría arreglármela? *seh meh ah rohtoh lah dehntahdoorah pohsteethah. pohdreeah arrehglahrmehlah?*

¿Qué diente/muela le duele?	Which tooth hurts?
Tiene un absceso	You've got an abscess
Tengo que tratarle el nervio	I'll have to do a root canal
Voy a ponerle anestesia local	I'm giving you a local anaesthetic
Tengo que empastarle/extraerle/ pulirle este/esta...	I'll have to fill/pull this tooth/file this...down
Tengo que usar el torno	I'll have to drill
Abra la boca	Open wide, please
Cierre la boca	Close your mouth, please
Enjuáguese	Rinse, please
¿Le sigue doliendo?	Does it hurt still?

In trouble

14 .1 Asking for help

Help!	¡Socorro!
	sohkohrroh!
Fire!	¡Fuego!
	fwehgoh!
Police!	¡Policía!
	pohleetheeah!
Quick!	¡Rápido!
	rahpeedoh!
Danger!	¡Peligro!
	pehleegroh!
Watch out!	¡Cuidado!
	kweedahdoh!
Stop!	¡Alto!
	ahltoh!
Be careful!	¡Cuidado!
	kweedahdoh!
Don't!	¡No, no!
	noh, noh!
Let go!	¡Suelte!
	swehlteh!
Stop that thief!	¡Al ladrón!
	ahl lahdrohn!
Could you help me, please?	¿Podría ayudarme, por favor?
	pohdreeah ahyoodahrmeh, pohr fahbohr?
Where's the police station/emergency exit/fire escape?	¿Dónde está la comisaría/la salida de emergencia/la escalera de incendios?
	dohndeh ehstah lah kohmeesahreeah/lah sahleedah deh ehmehrhehnthyah/lah ehskahlehrah deh eenthehndyohs?
Where's the nearest fire extinguisher?	¿Dónde hay un extintor?
	dohndeh ay oon ehxteentohr?
Call the fire brigade!	¡Llamen a los bomberos!
	lyahmehn ah lohs bohmbehrohs!
Call the police!	¡Llamen a la policía!
	lyahmehn ah lah pohleetheeah!
Call an ambulance!	¡Llamen a una ambulancia!
	lyahmehn ah oonah ahmboolahnthyah!
Where's the nearest phone?	¿Dónde hay un teléfono?
	dohndeh ay oon tehlehfohnoh?
Could I use your phone?	¿Podría llamar por teléfono?
	pohdreeah lyahmahr pohr tehlehfohnoh?
What's the emergency number?	¿Cuál es el número de urgencias?
	kwahl ehs ehl noomehroh deh oorhehnthyahs?
What's the number for the police?	¿Cuál es el número de la policía?
	kwahl ehs ehl noomehroh deh lah pohleetheeah?

I've lost my purse/_____ wallet	Se me ha perdido el monedero/la cartera *seh meh ah pehrdeedoh ehl* *mohnehdehroh/lah kahrtehrah*
I left my...behind _____ yesterday	Ayer me dejé el/la... *ahyehr meh deh**h**eh ehl/lah...*
I left my...here _____	Me he dejado el/la...aquí *meh eh deh**h**ahdoh ehl/lah...ahkee*
Did you find my...? _____	¿Han encontrado mi...? *ahn ehnkohntrahdoh mee...?*
It was right here_____	Estaba aquí *ehstahbah ahkee*
It's quite valuable _____	Es muy valioso *ehs mwee bahlyohsoh*
Where's the lost_____ property office?	¿Dónde está la oficina de objetos perdidos? *dohndeh ehstah lah ohfeetheenah deh* *ohb**h**ehtohs pehrdeedohs?*

There's been an _____ accident	Ha habido un accidente *ah ahbeedoh oon ahktheedehnteh*
Someone's fallen into _____ the water	Se ha caído alguien al agua *seh ah kaheedoh ahlghyehn ahl ahgwah*
There's a fire_____	Hay un incendio *ay oon eenthehndyoh*
Is anyone hurt? _____	¿Hay algún herido? *ay ahlgoon ehreedoh?*
Some people have _____ been/no one's been injured	(No) hay heridos *(noh) ay ehreedohs*
There's someone in _____ the car/train still	Todavía queda alguien en el coche/tren *tohdahbeeah kehdah ahlguyehn ehn ehl* *kohcheh/trehn*
It's not too bad. Don't_____ worry	No es grave. No se preocupe *noh ehs grahbeh. noh seh prehohkoopeh*
Leave everything the _____ way it is, please	No toque nada *noh tohkeh nahdah*
I want to talk to the_____ police first	Primero quisiera hablar con la policía *preemehroh keesyehrah ahblahr kohn lah* *pohleetheeah*
I want to take a _____ photo first	Primero quisiera sacar una foto *preemehroh keesyehrah sahkahr oonah* *fohtoh*
Here's my name_____ and address	Aquí tiene mi nombre y dirección *ahkee tyehneh mee nohmbreh ee* *deerehkthyohn*
Could I have your _____ name and address?	¿Me da su nombre y dirección? *meh dah soo nohmbreh ee deerehkthyohn?*
Could I see some_____ identification/your insurance papers?	¿Me permite su carnet de identidad/sus papeles del seguro? *meh pehrmeeteh soo kahrneh deh* *eedehnteedah/soos pahpehlehs dehl* *sehgooroh?*

In trouble

14

Will you act as a _____ witness?	¿Le importaría hacer de testigo? *leh eempohrtahreeah ahtehr deh tehsteegoh?*
I need the details for _____ the insurance	Necesito los datos para el seguro *nehthehseetoh lohs dahtohs pahrah ehl sehgooroh*
Are you insured? _____	¿Está asegurado? *ehstah ahsehgoorahdoh?*
Third party or _____ comprehensive?	¿Responsabilidad civil o contra todo riesgo? *rehspohnsahbeeleedahdh theebeel oh kohntrah tohdoh ryehsgoh?*
Could you sign here, _____ please?	Firme aquí, por favor *feermeh ahkee, pohr fahbohr*

🔴14 .4 Theft

I've been robbed _____	Me han robado *meh ahn rohbahdoh*
My...has been stolen _____	Me han robado el/la... *meh ahn rohbahdoh ehl/lah...*
My car's been _____ broken into	Me han abierto el coche *meh ahn ahbyehrtoh ehl kohcheh*

🔴14 .5 Missing person

I've lost my child/ _____ grandmother	Se ha perdido mi hijo/mi hija/mi abuela *seh ah pehrdeedoh mee eehoh/mee eehah/mee ahbwehlah*
Could you help me _____ find him/her?	¿Podría ayudarme a buscarlo/la? *pohdreeah ahyoodahrmeh ah booskahrloh/lah?*
Have you seen a _____ small child?	¿Ha visto a un niño pequeño/a una niña pequeña? *ah veestoh ah oon neenyoh pehkehnyoh/ah oonah neenyah pehkehnyah?*
He's/she's...years old _____	Tiene...años *tyehneh...ahnyohs*
He's/she's got _____ short/long/blond/red/ brown/black/ grey/curly/ straight/frizzy hair	corto/largo/rubio/rojo/castaño/negro/ canoso/rizado/liso/crespo *tyehneh ehl pehloh kohrtoh/lahrgoh/roobyoh/kahstahnyoh/neh groh/kahnohsoh/reethahdoh/leesoh/krehspoh*
with a ponytail _____	con cola de caballo *kohn kohlah deh kahbahlyoh*
with plaits _____	con trenzas *kohn trehnthahs*
in a bun _____	con moño *kohn mohnyoh*
He's/she's got _____ blue/brown/green eyes	Tiene ojos azules/marrones/verdes *tyehneh ohhohs ahthoolehs/mahrrohnehs/behrdehs*

He's wearing swimming ___ trunks/mountaineering boots	Lleva bañador/botas de montaña
	lyehbah bahnyahdohr/bohtahs deh mohntahnyah
with/without glasses/ _____ a bag	con/sin gafas/bolso
	kohn/seen gahfahs/bohlsoh
tall/short_____	alto/bajito
	ahltoh/bah__h__eetoh
This is a photo of _____ him/her	Esta es su foto
	ehstah ehs soo fohtoh
He/she must be lost _____	Seguramente se habrá perdido
	sehgoorahmehnteh seh ahbrah pehrdeedoh

14 .6 The police

An arrest

Los papeles del coche, por favor _____	**Your registration papers, please**
Conducía demasiado rápido _____	**You were speeding**
Tiene mal aparcado el coche_____	**You're not allowed to park here**
No ha puesto monedas en el _____ parquímetro	**You haven't put money in the meter**
No le funcionan los faros_____	**Your lights aren't working**
Le vamos a poner una multa de... _____ pesetas	**That's a...pesetas fine**
¿Va a pagar la multa en el acto? _____	**Do you want to pay on the spot?**
Tiene que pagar en el acto_____	**You'll have to pay on the spot**

I don't speak Spanish_____	No hablo español
	noh ahbloh ehspahnyohl
I didn't see the sign _____	No he visto el cartel
	noh eh beestoh ehl kahrtehl
I don't understand_____ what it says	No entiendo lo que dice
	noh ehntyehndoh loh keh deetheh
I was only doing..._____ kilometres an hour	Sólo iba a...kilómetros por hora
	sohloh eebah ah...keelohmehtrohs pohr ohrah
I'll have my car checked ___	Haré revisar el coche
	ahreh rehbeesahr ehl kohcheh
I was blinded by _____ oncoming lights	Me cegó un coche que venía de frente
	meh thehgoh oon kohcheh keh behneeah deh frehnteh

At the police station

I want to report a_____ collision/missing person/rape	Vengo a hacer la denuncia de un choque/un extravío/una violación
	behngoh ah ahthehr lah dehnoonthyah deh oon chohkeh/oon ehxtrahbeeoh/oonah beeohlahthyohn

Could you make out _____ a report, please?	¿Podría hacer un atestado?
	pohdreeah ahthehr oon ahtehstahdoh?
Could I have a copy _____ for the insurance?	¿Me podría dar una copia para el seguro?
	meh pohdreeah dahr oonah kohpyah pahrah ehl sehgooroh?
I've lost everything _____	He perdido todo
	eh pehrdeedoh tohdoh

¿Dónde ha sido? _____	Where did it happen?
¿Qué se le ha perdido? _____	What's missing?
¿Qué le han robado? _____	What's been taken?
¿Me permite su documento de_____ identidad?	Could I see some identification?
¿A qué hora ocurrió? _____	What time did it happen?
¿Quiénes estuvieron implicados? _____	Who was involved?
¿Hay testigos? _____	Are there any witnesses?
Rellene este formulario_____	Fill this out, please
Firme aquí, por favor_____	Sign here, please
¿Quiere un intérprete? _____	Do you want an interpreter?

I'd like an interpreter _____	Quisiera un intérprete
	keesyehrah oon eentehrprehteh
I'm innocent _____	Soy inocente
	soy eenohthehnteh
I don't know anything _____ about it	No sé nada
	noh seh nahdah
I want to speak to _____ someone...	Quisiera hablar con alguien de...
	keesyehrah ahblahr kohn ahlguyehn deh...
from the British _____ consulate	Quisiera hablar con alguien del Consulado Británico
	keesyehrah ahblahr kohn ahlguyehn dehl kohnsoolahdoh breetahneekoh
I need to see someone ____ from the British embassy	Quisiera hablar con alguien de la Embajada Británica
	keesyehrah ahblahr kohn ahlguyehn deh lah ehmbahhahdah breetahneekah
I want a lawyer who_____ speaks English	Quisiera un abogado que hable...
	keesyehrah oon ahbohgahdoh keh ahbleh...

In trouble

14

Word list

Word list English - Spanish

● **This word list** is meant to supplement the previous chapters.
Nouns are always accompanied by the Spanish definite article in order
to indicate whether it is a masculine (el) or feminine (la) word.
In a number of cases, words not contained in this list can be found
elsewhere in this booklet, namely alongside the diagrams of the car,
the bicycle and the tent. Many food terms can be found in the Spanish-
English list in 4.7.

A

a little	un poco	*oon pohkoh*
above (up)	arriba	*ahrreebah*
abroad	el extranjero	*ehl ehxtrahnhehroh*
accident	el accidente	*ehl ahktheedehnteh*
adder	la víbora	*la veebohrah*
addition	la suma	*lah soomah*
address	la dirección	*lah deerehkthyohn*
admission	la entrada	*lah ehntrahdah*
admission price	el precio de entrada	*ehl prehthyoh deh lah ehntrahdah*
admission ticket	la entrada	*lah ehntrahdah*
advice	el consejo	*ehl kohnsehhoh*
after	después de	*dehspwehs deh*
afternoon (in the)	(por) la tarde	*(pohr) lah tahrdeh*
aftershave	la loción para después del afeitado	*lah lohthyohn pahrah dehspwehs dehl ahfehytahdoh*
again	de nuevo	*deh nwehboh*
against	contra	*kohntrah*
age	la edad	*lah ehdahdh*
Aids	el Sida	*ehl seedah*
air conditioning	el aire acondicionado	*ehl ayreh ahkohndeethyohnahdoh*
air mattress	el colchón neumático	*ehl kohlchohn nehoomahteekoh*
air sickness bag	bolsita para el mareo	*bohlseetah pahrah ehl mahrehoh*
aircraft	el avión	*ehl ahbyohn*
airport	el aeropuerto	*ehl ahehrohpwehrtoh*
alarm	la alarma	*lah ahlahrmah*
alarm clock	el despertador	*ehl dehspehrtahdohr*
alcohol	el alcohol	*ehl ahlkohohl*
all the time	cada vez	*kahdah behth*
allergic	alérgico	*ahlehrheekoh*
alone	solo	*sohloh*
always	siempre	*syehmpreh*
ambulance	la ambulancia	*lah ahmboolahnthyah*
amount	el importe	*ehl eempohrteh*
amusement park	el parque de atracciones	*ehl pahrkeh deh ahtrahkthyohnehs*
anaesthetize	anestesiar	*ahnehstehsyahr*
anchovy	la anchoa	*lah ahnchohah*
angry	enfadado	*ehnfahdahdoh*
animal	el animal	*ehl ahneemahl*
ankle	el tobillo	*ehl tohbeelyoh*
answer	la respuesta	*lah rehspwehstah*

15

ant	la hormiga	*lah ohrmeegah*
antibiotics	los antibióticos	*lohs ahnteebyohteekohs*
antifreeze	el anticongelante	*ehl ahnteekohnhehlahnteh*
antique	antiguo	*ahnteegwoh*
antiques	las antigüedades	*lahs ahnteegwehdahdehs*
anus	el ano	*ehl ahnoh*
apartment	el apartamento	*ehl ahpahrtahmehntoh*
aperitif	el aperitivo	*ehl ahpehreeteeboh*
apologies	las disculpas	*lahs deeskoolpahs*
apple	la manzana	*lah mahnthahnah*
apple juice	el zumo de manzana	*ehl thoomoh deh mahnthahnah*
apple pie	la tarta de manzana	*lah tahrtah deh mahnthahnah*
apple sauce	el puré de manzanas	*ehl pooreh deh mahnthahnahs*
appointment	la hora	*lah ohrah*
approximately	más o menos	*mahs oh mehnohs*
April	abril	*ahbreel*
archbishop	el arzobispo	*ehl ahrthohbeespoh*
architecture	la arquitectura	*lah ahrkeetehktoorah*
area	los alrededores	*lohs ahlrehdehdohrehs*
arm	el brazo	*ehl brahthoh*
arrange to meet	quedar	*kehdahr*
arrive	llegar	*lyehgahr*
arrow	la flecha	*lah flehchah*
art	el arte	*ehl ahrteh*
artery	la arteria	*lah ahrtehryah*
artichokes	las alcachofas	*lahs ahlkahchohfahs*
article	el artículo	*ehl ahrteekooloh*
artificial respiration	la respiración artificial	*lah rehspeerahthyohn ahrteefeethyahl*
arts and crafts	la artesanía	*lah ahrtehsahneeah*
ashtray	el cenicero	*ehl thehneethehroh*
ask (a question)	preguntar	*prehgoontahr*
ask for	pedir	*pehdeer*
asparagus	los espárragos	*lohs ehspahrrahgohs*
aspirin	la aspirina	*lah ahspeereenah*
assault	la agresión	*lah ahgrehsyohn*
aubergine	la berenjena	*lah behrehnhehnah*
August	agosto	*ahgohstoh*
automatic	automático	*ahootohmahteekoh*
automatic car	el coche con cambio automático	*ehl kohcheh kohn kahmbyoh ahootohmahteekoh*
autumn	el otoño	*ehl ohtohnyoh*
avalanche	el alud	*ehl ahloodh*
awake (adj.)	despierto	*dehspyehrtoh*
awning	el toldo	*ehl tohldoh*

B

baby	el bebé	*ehl behbeh*
baby food	la comida para bebés	*lah kohmeedah pahrah behbehs*
babysitter	la niñera	*lah neenyehrah*
back (at the)	atrás	*ahtrahs*
back	la espalda	*lah ehspahldah*
backpack	la mochila	*lah mohcheelah*
bacon	el tocino	*ehl tohtheenoh*
bad	mal, malo	*mahl, mahloh*
bag	la bolsa	*lah bohlsah*
baker	la panadería	*lah pahnahdehreeah*
balcony (theatre)	el palco (alto)	*ehl pahlkoh (ahltoh)*
balcony (to building)	el balcón	*ehl bahlkohn*
ball	la pelota	*lah pehlohtah*
ballet	el ballet	*ehl bahleh*
ballpoint pen	el bolígrafo	*ehl bohleegrahfoh*
banana	el plátano	*ehl plahtahnoh*
bandage	la gasa	*lah gahsah*
bank (river)	la orilla	*lah ohreelyah*
bank	el banco	*ehl bahnkoh*
bank card	la tarjeta del banco	*lah tahrhehtah dehl bahnkoh*
bar (café)	el bar	*ehl bahr*
bar (drinks' cabinet)	la barra	*lah bahrrah*
bar	la barra	*lah bahrrah*
barbecue	la barbacoa	*lah bahrbahkohah*
basketball	el baloncesto	*ehl bahlohnthehstoh*
bath	el baño	*ehl bahnyoh*
bath attendant	el bañista	*ehl bahnyeestah*
bath foam	el gel de baño	*ehl hehl deh bahnyoh*
bath towel	la toalla de baño	*lah tohahlyah deh bahnyoh*
bathing cap	el gorro de baño	*ehl gohrroh deh bahnyoh*
bathing cubicle	la caseta	*lah kahsehtah*
bathing suit	el bañador	*ehl bahnyahdohr*
bathroom	el cuarto de baño	*ehl kwahrtoh deh bahnyoh*
battery (car)	la batería	*lah bahtehreeah*
battery	la pila	*lah peelah*
beach	la playa	*lah plahyah*
beans	las judías blancas	*lahs hoodeeahs blahnkahs*
beautiful	bonito	*bohneetoh*
beauty parlour	el salón de belleza	*ehl sahlohn deh behlyehthah*
bed	la cama	*lah kahmah*
bee	la abeja	*lah ahbehhah*
beef	la carne de vaca	*lah kahrneh deh bahkah*
beer	la cerveza	*lah thehrbehthah*
beetroot	la remolacha	*lah rehmohlahchah*
begin	empezar	*ehmpehthahr*
beginner	el principiante	*ehl preentheepyahnteh*
behind	atrás	*ahtrahs*
Belgian (f)	la belga	*lah behlgah*
Belgian (m)	el belga	*ehl behlgah*

Belgium	Bélgica	*behlheekah*
bellboy	el mozo de cuerda	*ehl mohthoh deh kwehrdah*
belt	el cinturón	*ehl theentoorohn*
berth	la litera	*lah leetehrah*
better	mejor	*mehhohr*
bicarb	el bicarbonato	*ehl beekahrbohnahtoh*
bicycle	la bicicleta	*lah beetheeklehtah*
bicycle pump	el inflador	*ehl eenflahdohr*
bicycle repairman	el mecánico de bicicletas	*ehl mehkahneekoh deh beetheeklehtahs*
bikini	el bikini	*ehl beekeenee*
bill	la cuenta	*lah kwehntah*
billiards, to play	el juego de billar	*ehl hwehgoh deh beelyahr*
birthday (to have a)	cumplir años	*koompleer ahnyohs*
birthday	el cumpleaños	*ehl koomplehahnyohs*
biscuit	la galleta	*lah gahlyehtah*
bite	morder	*mohrdehr*
bitter	amargo	*ahmahrgoh*
black	negro	*nehgroh*
bland	soso	*sohsoh*
blanket	la manta	*lah mahntah*
bleach	teñir de rubio	*tehnyeer deh roobyoh*
blister	la ampolla	*lah ahmpohlyah*
blond	rubio	*roobyoh*
blood	la sangre	*lah sahngreh*
blood pressure	la tensión sanguínea	*lah tehnsyohn sahngheenehah*
blouse	la blusa	*lah bloosah*
blow dry	secar a mano	*sehkahr ah mahnoh*
blue	azul	*ahthool*
boat	el barco	*ehl bahrkoh*
body	el cuerpo	*ehl kwehrpoh*
body milk	la leche corporal	*lah lehcheh kohrpohrahl*
boiled	cocido	*kohtheedoh*
boiled ham	el jamón de York	*ehl hahmohn deh yohrk*
bonbon	el bombón	*ehl bohmbohn*
bone	el hueso	*ehl wehsoh*
bonnet	el capó	*ehl kahpoh*
book (verb)	reservar	*rehsehrbahr*
book	el libro	*ehl leebroh*
booked	reservado	*rehsehrbahdah*
booking office	la taquilla	*lah tahkeelyah*
bookshop	la librería	*lah leebrehreeah*
border	la frontera	*lah frohntehrah*
bored (be)	aburrirse	*ahboorreerseh*
boring	aburrido	*ahboorreedoh*
born	nacido	*nahtheedoh*
botanical gardens	el jardín botánico	*ehl hahrdeen bohtahneekoh*
both	ambos/ambas	*ahmbohs/ahmbahs*
bottle (baby's)	el biberón	*ehl beebehrohn*
bottle	la botella	*lah bohtehlyah*
bottle-warmer	el calentador de biberones	*ehl kahlehntahdohr de beebehrohnehs*
box (in theatre)	el palco	*ehl pahlkoh*

box	la caja	*kahhah*
boy	el chico	*ehl cheekoh*
bra	el sujetador	*ehl soohehtahdohr*
bracelet	la pulsera	*lah poolsehrah*
braised	estofado	*ehstohfahdoh*
brake	el freno	*ehl frehnoh*
brake fluid	el líquido de frenos	*ehl leekeedoh deh frehnohs*
bread	el pan	*ehl pahn*
bread roll	el panecillo	*ehl pahnehtheelyoh*
breakdown recovery	el auxilio en carretera	*ehl ahooxeelyoh ehn kahrrehtehrah*
break (limb)	fracturarse	*frahktoorahrseh*
breakfast	el desayuno	*ehl dehsahyoonoh*
breast	el pecho	*ehl pehchoh*
bridge	el puente	*ehl pwehnteh*
bring	llevar	*lyehbahr*
brochure	el folleto	*ehl fohlyehtoh*
broken	roto, estropeado	*rohtoh, ehstrohpehahdoh*
broth	el caldo	*ehl kahldoh*
brother	el hermano	*ehl ehrmahnoh*
brown	marrón	*mahrrohn*
bruise (verb)	contusionarse	*kohntoosyohnahrseh*
brush	el cepillo	*ehl thehpeelyoh*
Brussels sprouts	las coles de Bruselas	*lahs kohlehs deh broosehlahs*
bucket	el cubo	*ehl kooboh*
bug	el bicho	*ehl beechoh*
building	el edificio	*ehl ehdeefeethyoh*
bullfight	la corrida de toros	*lah kohrreedah deh tohrohs*
buoy	la boya	*lah boyah*
burglary	el robo en una casa	*ehl rohboh ehn oonah kahsah*
burn (verb)	quemar	*kehmahr*
burn	la quemadura	*lah kehmahdoorah*
burnt	quemado	*kehmahdoh*
bus	el autobús	*ehl ahootohboos*
bus station	la estación de autobuses	*lah ehstahthyohn deh ahootohboosehs*
bus stop	la parada de autobús	*lah pahrahdah deh ahootohboosehs*
business class	la clase preferente	*lah klahseh prehfehrehnteh*
business trip	el viaje de negocios	*ehl byahheh deh nehgohthyohs*
busy (crowded)	hay mucha gente	*ay moochah hehnteh*
butane camping gas	el gas butano	*ehl gahs bootahnoh*
butcher's	la carnicería	*lah kahrneethehreeah*
butter	la mantequilla	*lah mahntehkeelyah*
button	el botón	*ehl bohtohn*
buy	comprar	*kohmprahr*
by airmail	el correo aéreo/ vía aérea	*ehl kohrrehoh ahehrehoh/beeah ahehrehah*

c

cabbage	la col, la berza	*lah kohl, lah behrthah*
cabin	la cabaña	*lah kahbahnyah*
cake	el pastel	*ehl pahstehl*
cake shop	la pastelería, la confitería	*lah pahstehlehreeah, lah kohnfeetehreeah*
call (by phone)	llamar por teléfono	*lyahmahr pohr tehlehfohnoh*
called, to be	llamarse	*lyahmahrseh*
camera	la máquina fotográfica	*lah mahkeenah fohtohgrahfeekah*
camp	acampar	*ahkahmpahr*
camp shop	la tienda del camping	*lah tyehndah dehl kahmpeen*
camp site	el camping	*ehl kahmpeen*
camper van	el autocaravana	*ehl ahootohkahrah-bahnnah*
campfire	la fogata	*lah fohgahtah*
camping guide	la guía de camping	*lah gheeah deh kahmpeen*
camping permit	el permiso de acampar	*ehl pehrmeesoh deh ahkahmpahr*
canal boat	el barco de excursión	*ehl bahrkoh deh ehxkoorsyohn*
cancel	cancelar	*kahnthehlahr*
candle	la vela	*lah behlah*
canoe	la piragua	*lah peerahgwah*
canoeing	el piragüismo	*ehl peerahgweesmoh*
cap (hat)	el gorro	*ehl gohrroh*
car	el coche	*ehl kohcheh*
car deck	la bodega para coches	*lah bohdehgah pahrah kohchehs*
car documents	los papeles del coche	*lohs pahpehlehs dehl kohcheh*
car registration	el permiso de circulación	*ehl pehrmeesoh deh theerkoolahthyohn*
car trouble	la avería	*lah ahbehreeah*
carafe	la jarra	*lah hahrrah*
caravan	la caravana	*lah kahrahbahnah*
cardigan	el chaleco	*ehl chahlehkoh*
careful	con cuidado	*kohn kweedahdoh*
carrot	la zanahoria	*lah thahnahohryah*
carton	el cartón	*ehl kahrtohn*
cartridge	el carrete de cassette	*ehl kahrrehteh deh kahseht*
cascade	la cascada	*lah kahskahdah*
cash desk	la caja	*lah kahhah*
casino	el casino	*ehl kahseenoh*
cassette	la cassette	*lah kahseht*
castle	el castillo	*ehl kahsteelyoh*
cat	el gato	*ehl gahtoh*
catalogue	el catálogo	*ehl kahtahlohgoh*
cathedral	la catedral	*lah kahtehdrahl*
cauliflower	la coliflor	*lah kohleeflohr*
cave	la gruta	*lah grootah*
CD	el compact disc	*ehl kohmpahkt deesk*

Word list

15

celebrate	celebrar una fiesta	*thehlehbrahr oonah fyehsta*
cellotape	la celo	*lah thehloh*
cemetery	el cementerio	*ehl thehmehntehryoh*
centimetre	centímetro(s)	*thehnteemehtroh(s)*
central heating	la calefacción central	*lah kahlehfakthyohn thehntrahl*
centre (in the)	en el centro/ medio	*ehn ehl thehntroh/ mehdyoh*
centre	el centro	*ehl thehntroh*
chair	la silla	*lah seelyah*
chambermaid	la camarera	*lah kahmahrehrah*
chamois	la gamuza	*lah gahmoothah*
champagne	el champán/el cava	*ehl chahmpahn/ehl kahbah*
change (from paying)	la vuelta	*lah bwehltah*
change (train/plane etc.)	hacer trasbordo	*ahthehr trahsbohrdoh*
change (verb)	cambiar	*kahmbyahr*
change the baby's nappy	cambiar los pañales	*kahmbyahr lohs pahnyahlehs*
change the oil	cambiar el aceite	*kahmbyahr ehl ahtheyteh*
chapel	la capilla	*lah kahpeelyah*
charter flight	el vuelo chárter	*ehl bwehloh chahrtehr*
chat up	ligar	*leegahr*
check (verb)	controlar	*kohntrohlahr*
check in	facturar	*frahktoorahr*
cheers	salud	*sahloodh*
cheese (tasty, mild)	el queso (añejo, blando)	*ehl kehsoh (ahnyeh<u>h</u>oh,blahndoh)*
chef	el jefe	*ehl <u>h</u>ehfeh*
chemist	la droguería	*lah drohguehreeah*
cheque	el cheque	*ehl chehkeh*
cherries	las cerezas	*lahs thehrehthahs*
chess (play)	jugar al ajedrez	*<u>h</u>oogahr ahl a<u>h</u>ehdreth*
chewing gum	el chicle	*ehl cheekleh*
chicken	el pollo	*ehl pohlyoh*
chicory	las endivias	*lahs ehndeebyahs*
child	el hijo, el niño	*ehl ee<u>h</u>oh, ehl neenyoh*
child seat	el asiento para niños	*ehl ahsyehntoh pahrah neenyohs*
child's seat	el sillín para niños	*ehl seelyeen pahrah neenyohs*
chilled	refrigerado	*rehfree<u>h</u>ehrahdoh*
chin	la barbilla	*lah bahrbeelyah*
chips/crisps	las patatas fritas	*lahs pahtahtahs freetahs*
chocolate	el chocolate	*ehl chohkohlahteh*
choose	elegir/escoger	*ehleh<u>h</u>eer/ehskoh<u>h</u>ehr*
chop	la chuleta	*la choolehtah*
christian name	el nombre	*ehl nohmbreh*
church	la iglesia	*lah eeglehsyah*
church service	el servicio religioso	*ehl sehrbeethyoh rehlee<u>h</u>yohsoh*
cigar	el puro	*ehl pooroh*
cigar shop	el estanco	*ehl ehstahnkoh*
cigarette	el cigarrillo	*ehl theegahrreelyoh*

cigarette paper	el papel de fumar	*ehl pahpehl deh foomahr*
cine camera	la filmadora	*lah feelmahdohrah*
circle	el círculo	*ehl theerkooloh*
circus	el circo	*ehl theerkoh*
city map	el plano	*ehl plahnoh*
classic/classical	clásica	*klahseekah*
clean (adj.)	limpio	*leempyoh*
clean (verb)	limpiar	*leempyahr*
clear (adj.)	claro	*klahroh*
clearance	la liquidación	*lah leekeedahthyohn*
closed	cerrado	*thehrrahdoh*
closed off	(la carretera) cerrada	*(lah kahrrehtehrah) thehrrahdah*
clothes	la ropa	*lah rohpah*
clothes hanger	la percha	*lah pehrchah*
clothes peg	la pinza para la ropa	*lah peenthah pahrah lah rohpah*
coat	el abrigo	*ehl ahbreegoh*
cockroach	la cucaracha	*lah kookahrahchah*
cod	el bacalao (fresco)	*ehl bahkahlahoh (frehskoh)*
coffee	el café	*ehl kahfeh*
coffee creamer	la crema para el café	*lah krehmah pahrah ehl kahfeh*
coffee filter	el filtro de café	*ehl feeltroh deh kahfeh*
cognac	el coñac	*ehl kohnyah*
cold	frío	*freeoh*
cold	el constipado	*ehl kohnsteepahdoh*
cold cuts	los fiambres	*lohs fyahmbrehs*
collarbone	la clavícula	*lah klahbeekoolah*
colleague	el/la colega	*ehl/lah kohlehgah*
collision	el choque	*ehl chohkeh*
cologne	el agua de tocador	*ehl ahgwah deh tohkahdohr*
colour	el color	*ehl kohlohr*
colour TV	el televisor color	*ehl tehlehbeesohr kohlohr*
coloured pencils	los lápices de colores	*lohs lahpeethehs deh kohlohrehs*
colouring book	el libro para colorear	*ehl leebroh pahrah kohlohrehahr*
comb	el peine	*ehl peheeneh*
come	venir	*behneer*
compartment	el compartimiento	*ehl kohmpahrteemyehntoh*
complaint (medical)	la molestia	*lah mohlehstyah*
complaint	la queja	*lah kehhah*
complaints book	el libro de reclamaciones	*ehl leebroh deh rehklahmahthyohnehs*
completely	del todo	*dehl tohdoh*
compliment	el cumplido	*ehl koompleedoh*
compulsory	obligatorio	*ohbleegahtohryoh*
concert	el concierto	*ehl kohnthyehrtoh*
concert hall	la sala de conciertos	*lah sahlah deh kohnthyehrtohs*

concussion	la conmoción cerebral	lah kohnmohthyohn thehrehbrahl
condiments	los condimentos	lohs kohndeemehntohs
condom	el condón	ehl kohndohn
congratulate	felicitar	fehleetheetahr
connection	el enlace	ehl ehnlahtheh
constipation	el estreñimiento	ehl ehstrehnyeemyehntoh
consulate	el consulado	ehl kohnsoolahdoh
consultation	la consulta	lah kohnsooltah
contact lens	la lentilla	lah lehnteelyah
contact lens solution	el líquido para las lentillas	ehl leekeedoh pahrah lahs lehnteelyahs
contagious	contagioso	kohntah_h_yohsoh
contest	el concurso	ehl kohnkoorsoh
contraceptive	el anticonceptivo	ehl ahnteekohn-thehpteeboh
contraceptive pill	la píldora anticonceptiva	ah peeldohrah lahnteekohnthehpteebah
convent	el convento	ehl kohnbehntoh
cook (verb)	cocinar	kohtheenahr
cook	el cocinero	ehl kohtheenehroh
copper	el cobre	ehl kohbreh
copy	la copia	lah kohpyah
corkscrew	el sacacorchos	ehl sahkahkohrchohs
corn flour	la maicena	lah maheethehnah
corner	el rincón	ehl reenkohn
correct	correcto	kohrrehktoh
correspond	cartearse	kahrtehahrseh
corridor	el pasillo	ehl pahseelyoh
costume	el traje	ehl trah_h_eh
cot	la cuna	lah koonah
cotton	el algodón	ehl ahlgohdohn
cotton wool	el algodón	ehl ahlgohdohn
cough	la tos	lah tohs
cough mixture	el jarabe para la tos	ehl _h_ahrahbeh pahrah lah tohs
counter	el mostrador	ehl mohstrahdohr
country	el país	ehl pahees
country code	el indicativo del país	ehl eendeekahteeboh dehl pahees
country(side)	el campo	ehl kahmpoh
courgette	el calabacín	ehl kahlahbahtheen
course (of treatment)	la cura	lah koorah
cousin (f)	la prima	lah preemah
cousin (m)	el primo	ehl preemoh
crab	el cangrejo	ehl kahngre_h_oh
cream	la crema, la nata	lah krehmah, lah nahtah
credit card	la tarjeta de crédito	lah tahr_h_ehtah deh krehdeetoh
crisps/chips	las patatas fritas	lahs pahtahtahs freetahs
croissant	el croissant	ehl krwahsahn
cross the road	cruzar la calle	kroothahr lah kahlyeh
cross-country run	la pista de esquí de fondo	lah peestah deh ehskee deh fohndoh

cross-country skiing	el esquí de fondo	ehl ehskee deh fohndoh
cross-country skis	los esquís de fondo	lohs ehskees deh fohndóh
crossing (journey)	la travesía	lah trahbehseeah
cry (verb)	llorar	lyohrahr
cubic metre(s)	metro(s) cúbico(s)	mehtroh(s) koobeekoh(s)
cucumber	el pepino	ehl pehpeenoh
cuddly toy	el animal de peluche	ehl ahneemahl deh pehloocheh
cuff links	los gemelos	lohs _h_ehmehlohs
culottes	la falda-pantalón	lah fahldah pahntahlohn
cup	la taza	lah tahthah
curly	rizado	reethahdoh
current	la corriente	lah kohrryehnteh
cushion	el cojín	ehl coh_h_een
custard	las natillas	lahs nahteelyahs
customary	habitual	ahbeetwahl
customs	la aduana	lah ahdwahna
customs check	el control de aduanas	ehl kohntrohl deh ahdwahnahs
cut (verb)	cortar	kohrtahr
cutlery	los cubiertos	lohs koobyehrtohs
cycling	montar en bicicleta	mohntahr ehn beetheeklehtah

D

dairy products	los productos lácteos	lohs prodooktohs lahktehohs
damaged	dañado, estropeado	dahnyahdoh, ehstrohpehahdoh
dance	bailar	bahylahr
dandruff	la caspa	lah kahspah
danger	el peligro	ehl pehleegroh
dangerous	peligroso	pehleegrohsoh
dark	oscuro	ohskooroh
date	la cita	lah theetah
daughter	la hija	lah ee_h_ah
day	el día, las 24 horas	ehl deeah, lahs beheenteekwahtroh ohrahs
day before yesterday	anteayer	ahnteahyehr
dead	muerto	mwehrtoh
decaffeinated	sin cafeína	seen kahfeheenah
December	diciembre	deethyehmbreh
deck chair	el sillón de playa	ehl seelyohn deh plahyah
declare(customs)	declarar	dehklahrahr
deep	hondo	ohndoh
deep sea diving	el buceo	ehl boothehoh
degrees	los grados	lohs grahdohs
delay	el retraso	ehl rehtrahsoh
delicious	delicioso	dehleethyohsoh
dentist	el dentista	ehl dehnteestah
dentures	la dentadura postiza	lah dehntahdoorah pohsteethah

deodorant	el desodorante	*ehl dehsohdohrahnteh*
department	la sección	*lah sehkthyohn*
department stores	los grandes almacenes	*lohs grahndehs ahlmahthehnehs*
departure	la partida	*lah pahrteedah*
departure time	la hora de salida	*lah ohrah deh sahleedah*
depilatory cream	la crema depilatoria	*lah krehmah dehpeelahtohryah*
deposit (in)	en consigna	*ehn kohnseegnah*
deposit	la fianza	*lah fyahnzah*
dessert	el postre	*ehl pohstreh*
destination	el destino, el punto final	*ehl dehsteenoh, ehl poontoh feenahl*
develop (photos)	revelar	*rehbehlahr*
diabetic	el diabético	*ehl dyahbehteekoh*
dial (verb)	marcar	*mahrkahr*
diamond	el diamante	*ehl deeahmahnteh*
diarrhoea	la diarrea	*lah deeahrrehah*
dictionary	el diccionario	*ehl deekthyohnahryoh*
diesel	el gasóleo	*ehl gahsohlehoh*
diet	la dieta	*lah dyehtah*
difficulty	la dificultad	*lah deefeekooltahdh*
dining room	el comedor	*ehl kohmehdohr*
dining/buffet car	el coche restaurante	*ehl kohcheh rehstahoorahnteh*
dinner (to have)	cenar	*thehnahr*
dinner	la cena, la comida	*lah thehnah, lah kohmeedah*
dinner jacket	el smoking	*ehl smohkeen*
direction	la dirección	*lah deerehkthyohn*
directly	directo	*deerehktoh*
dirty	sucio	*soothyoh*
disabled person	el minusválido	*ehl meenoosbahleedoh*
disappearance	la desaparición	*lah dehsahpahreethyohn*
disco	la discoteca	*lah deeskohtehkah*
discount	el descuento	*ehl dehskwehntoh*
dish	el plato	*ehl plahtoh*
dish of the day	el plato del día	*ehl plahtoh dehl deeah*
disinfectant	el desinfectante	*ehl dehseenfehktahnteh*
distance	la distancia	*lah deestahnthyah*
distilled water	el agua destilada	*ehl ahgwah dehsteelahdah*
disturb	molestar	*mohlehstahr*
disturbance	el fallo	*ehl fahlyoh*
dive (verb)	bucear	*boothehahr*
diving	el buceo	*ehl boothehoh*
diving board	el trampolín	*ehl trahmpohleen*
diving gear	el equipo de buzo	*ehl ehkeepoh deh boothoh*
divorced	divorciado	*deebohrthyahdoh*
DIY-shop	la tienda de artículos de bricolaje	*lah tyehndah deh ahrteekoolohs deh breekohlaheh*
dizzy	mareado	*mahrehahdoh*

do (verb)	hacer	ahthehr
doctor	el médico	ehl mehdeekoh
dog	el perro	ehl pehrroh
doll	la muñeca	lah moonyehkah
domestic	nacionales	nahtheeohnahlehs
done	hecho	ehchoh
door	la puerta	lah pwehrtah
double	doble	dohbleh
down	abajo	ahbahhoh
draught (to be a)	haber corriente	ahbehr kohrryehnteh
draughts (play)	jugar a las damas	hoogahr ah lahs dahmahs
dream	soñar	sohnyahr
dress	el vestido	ehl behsteedoh
dressing gown	la bata	lah bahtah
drink (verb)	beber	behbehr
drinking chocolate	el chocolate	ehl chohkohlahteh
drinking water	el agua potable	ehl ahgwah pohtahbleh
drive (verb)	ir en coche	eer ehn kohcheh
driver	el chófer	ehl chohfehr
driving licence	el permiso de conducir	ehl pehrmeesoh deh kohndootheer
drought	la sequía	lah sehkeeah
dry (verb)	secar	sehkahr
dry	seco	sehkoh
dry clean	lavar en seco	lahbahr ehn sehkoh
dry cleaner's	la tintorería	lah teentohrehreeah
dry shampoo	el champú seco	ehl chahmpoo sehkoh
dummy	el chupete	ehl choopehteh
during	durante	doorahnteh
during the day	de día	deh deeah

E

ear	la oreja	lah ohrehhah
ear, nose and throat (ENT) specialist	el médico de oídos	ehl mehdeekoh deh oheedohs
earache	el dolor de oído	ehl dohlohr deh oheedoh
eardrops	las gotas para los oídos	lahs gohtahs pahrah lohs oheedohs
early	temprano	tehmprahnoh
earrings	los pendientes	lohs pehndyehntehs
earth	la tierra	lah tyehrrah
earthenware	la cerámica	lah thehrahmeekah
east	el este	ehl ehsteh
easy	fácil	fahtheel
eat	comer	kohmehr
eczema	el eczema	ehl ehkthehmah
eel	la anguila	lah ahngueelah
egg	el huevo	ehl wehboh
elastic band	la goma elástica	lah gohmah ehlahsteekah
electric	eléctrico	ehlehktreekoh
electricity	la corriente	lah kohrryehnteh
embassy	la embajada	lah ehmbahhahdah
emergency brake	el freno de emergencia	ehl frehnoh deh ehmehrhehnthyah

Word list

15

emergency exit	la salida de emergencia	lah sahleedah deh ehmehr<u>r</u>ehnthyah
emergency number	el número de urgencias	ehl noomehroh deh oor<u>r</u>ehnthyahs
emergency phone	el teléfono de emergencia	ehl tehlehfohnoh deh ehmehr<u>r</u>ehnthyah
emergency triangle	el triángulo reflectante	ehl treeahngooloh rehflehktahnteh
emery board	la lima (para uñas)	lah leemah (pahrah oonyahs)
empty	vacío	bahtheeoh
engaged (phone)	comunicando	kohmooneekahndoh
engaged	ocupado	ohkoopahdoh
English	inglés	eenglehs
enjoy	disfrutar	deesfrootahr
entertainment guide	la guía de los espectáculos	lah gheeah deh lohs ehspehktahkoolohs
envelope	el sobre	ehl sohbreh
escort	el/la acompañante	ehl/lah ahkohmpahnyahnteh
evening	la tarde	lah tahrdeh
evening wear	el traje de etiqueta	ehl trah<u>h</u>eh deh ehteekehtah
event	el acontecimiento	ehl akohntehthee-myehntoh
event (social)	la función	lah foonthyohn
everything	todo	tohdoh
everywhere	en todas partes	ehn tohdahs pahrtehs
examine	reconocer	rehkohnohthehr
excavation	las excavaciones	lahs ehxkahbahthyohnehs
excellent	excelente, estupendo	ehxthehlehnteh, ehstoopehndoh
exchange (verb)	cambiar	kahmbyahr
exchange office	la oficina de cambio	lah ohfeetheenah deh kahmbyoh
exchange rate	la cotización, el tipo de cambio	lah kohteethahthyohn, ehl teepoh deh kahmbyoh
excursion	la excursión organizada	lah ehxkoorsyohn ohrgahneethahdah
exhibition	la exposición	lah ehxpohseethyohn
exit	la salida	lah sahleedah
expenses	los gastos	lohs gahstohs
expensive	caro	kahroh
explain	explicar	ehxpleekahr
express train	el tren rápido	ehl trehn rahpeedoh
external	tópico, externo	tohpeekoh, ehxtehrnoh
eye	el ojo	ehl oh<u>h</u>oh
eye drops	las gotas para los ojos	lahs gohtahs pahrah lohs oh<u>h</u>ohs
eye shadow	la sombra de ojos	lah sohmbrah deh oh<u>h</u>ohs
eye specialist	el oculista	ehl ohkooleestah
eyeliner	el lápiz de ojos	ehl lahpeeth deh oh<u>h</u>ohs

F

face	la cara	*lah kahrah*
factory	la fábrica	*lah fahbreekah*
fair	la feria	*lah fehryah*
fall	caer(se)	*kahehr(seh)*
family	la familia	*lah fahmeelyah*
famous	famoso	*fahmohsoh*
far away	lejos	*leh<u>h</u>ohs*
farm	la granja	*lah grahn<u>h</u>ah*
farmer	el campesino	*ehl kahmpehseenoh*
farmer's wife	la campesina	*lah kahmpehseenah*
fashion	la moda	*lah mohdah*
fast	rápido	*rahpeedoh*
father	el padre	*ehl pahdreh*
fault (blame)	la culpa	*lah koolpah*
fax (verb)	enviar un fax	*ehnbyahr oon fahx*
February	febrero	*fehbrehroh*
feel (verb)	sentir	*sehnteer*
feel like	apetecer	*ahpehtehthehr*
fence	la verja	*lah behr<u>h</u>ah*
ferry	el transbordador	*ehl trahnsbohrdahdohr*
fever	la fiebre	*lah fyehbreh*
fill (tooth)	empastar	*ehmpahstahr*
fill out	rellenar	*rehlyehnahr*
filling	el empaste	*ehl ehmpahsteh*
film (camera)	el rollo	*ehl rohlyoh*
film	la película	*lah pehleekoolah*
filter	el filtro	*ehl feeltroh*
find (verb)	encontrar	*ehnkohntrahr*
fine	la multa	*lah mooltah*
finger	el dedo	*ehl dehdoh*
fire	el fuego	*ehl fwehgoh*
fire (house etc.)	el incendio	*ehl eenthehndyoh*
fire brigade	los bomberos	*lohs bohmbehrohs*
fire escape	la escalera de incendios	*lah ehskahlehrah deh eenthehndyohs*
fire extinguisher	el extintor	*ehl ehxteentohr*
first	primero	*preemehroh*
first aid	los primeros auxilios	*lohs preemehrohs ahooxeelyohs*
first class	la primera clase	*lah preemehrah klahseh*
fish (verb)	pescar	*pehskahr*
fish	el pescado	*ehl pehskahdoh*
fishing rod	la caña de pescar	*lah kanyah deh pehskahr*
fitness centre	el gimnasio	*ehl <u>h</u>eemnahsyoh*
fitness training	la gimnasia	*lah <u>h</u>eemnahsyah*
fitting room	el probador	*ehl prohbahdohr*
fix puncture	arreglar el pinchazo	*ahrrehglahr ehl peenchahthoh*
flag	la bandera	*lah bahndehrah*
flamenco	el flamenco	*ehl flahmehnkoh*
flash cube	el cuboflash	*ehl koobohflahsh*
flash gun/bulb	el flash	*ehl flahsh*
flat	el piso	*ehl peesoh*

Word list

15

127

flea market	el mercadillo, el rastro	*ehl mehrkahdeelyoh, ehl rahstroh*
flight	el vuelo	*ehl bwehloh*
flight number	el número de vuelo	*ehl noomehroh deh bwehloh*
flood	la inundación	*lah eenoondathyohn*
floor	el piso	*ehl peesoh*
flour	la harina	*lah ahreenah*
flu	la gripe	*lah greepeh*
fly (insect)	la mosca	*lah mohskah*
fly (verb)	volar	*bohlahr*
fly-over	el viaducto	*ehl beeahdooktoh*
fog	la niebla	*lah nyehblah*
foggy (be)	haber niebla	*ahbehr nyehblah*
folkloristic	folclórico	*fohlklohreekoh*
follow	seguir	*sehgueer*
food	el alimento	*ehl ahleemehntoh*
food poisoning	la intoxicación alimenticia	*lah eentohxeekaht-hyohn ahleemehntee-thyah*
foodstuffs	los víveres	*lohs beebehrehs*
foot	el pie	*ehl pyeh*
for	antes, delante de	*ahntehs, dehlahnteh deh*
for hire	se alquila	*seh ahlkeelah*
forbidden	prohibido	*proheebeedoh*
forehead	la frente	*lah frehnteh*
foreign	extranjero	*ehxtrahnhehroh*
forget	olvidar	*ohlbeedahr*
fork	el tenedor	*ehl tehnehdohr*
form	el formulario	*ehl fohrmoolahryoh*
fort	la fortificación	*lah fohrteefeekah-thyohn*
forward (send)	enviar	*ehnbyahr*
fountain	la fuente	*lah fwehnteh*
four-star petrol	súper	*soopehr*
frame	la montura	*lah mohntoorah*
free	libre	*leebreh*
free of charge	gratuito	*grahtweetoh*
free time	el tiempo libre	*ehl tyehmpoh leebreh*
freeze	helar	*ehlahr*
French	francés	*frahnthehs*
French bread	la barra de pan	*lah bahrrah deh pahn*
fresh	fresco	*frehskoh*
Friday	el viernes	*ehl byehrnehs*
fried	frito	*freetoh*
fried egg	el huevo al plato	*ehl wehboh ahl plahtoh*
friend	el amigo	*ehl ahmeegoh*
friendly	cordial, amable	*kohrdyahl, ahmahbleh*
frightened	miedoso	*myehdohsoh*
fringe	el flequillo	*ehl flehkeelyoh*
front (at the)	adelante	*ahdehlahnteh*
frozen goods	los productos congelados	*los prohdooktohs kohnhehlahdohs*
fruit	la fruta	*lah frootah*
fruit juice	el zumo de frutas	*ehl thoomoh deh frootahs*

frying pan	la sartén	*lah sahrtehn*
full	lleno	*lyehnoh*
fun	la diversión	*lah deebehrsyohn*

G

gallery	la galería de arte	*lah gahlehreeah deh ahrteh*
game	el juego	*el hwehgoh*
garage (for repairs)	el taller mecánico	*ehl tahlyehr mehkahneekoh*
garbage bag	la bolsa de basura	*lah bohlsah deh bahsoorah*
garden	el jardín	*ehl hahrdeen*
gastroenteritis	la gastroenteritis	*lah gahstrohehnteh-reetees*
gauze	la gasa esterilizada	*lah gahsah ehstehreeleethahdah*
gear (bicycle)	el cambio	*ehl kahmbyoh*
gel	el gel	*ehl hehl*
German	alemán	*ahlehmahn*
get married	casarse	*kahsahrse*
get off	bajarse	*bahhahrse*
gift	el regalo	*ehl rehgahloh*
gilt	dorado	*dohrahdoh*
ginger	el jengibre	*ehl hehnheebreh*
girl	la chica	*lah cheekah*
girlfriend	la amiga	*lah ahmeegah*
giro card	la tarjeta de la caja postal	*lah tahrhehtah deh lah kahhah pohstahl*
giro cheque	el cheque postal	*ehl chehkeh pohstahl*
glacier	el glaciar	*ehl glahthyahr*
glass (tumbler)	el vaso	*ehl bahsoh*
glass (wine -)	la copa	*lah kohpah*
glasses	las gafas	*lahs gahfahs*
glider	el vuelo sin motor	*ehl bwehloh seen mohtohr*
glove	el guante	*ehl gwahnteh*
glue	la cola	*lah kohlah*
gnat	el mosquito	*ehl mohskeetoh*
go (verb)	ir	*eer*
go back, come back	volver	*bohlbehr*
go backwards	ir para atrás	*eer pahrah ahtrahs*
go out	salir	*sahleer*
goat's cheese	el queso de cabra	*ehl kehsoh deh kahbrah*
gold	el oro	*ehl ohroh*
golf	el golf	*ehl gohlf*
golf course	el campo de golf	*ehl kahmpoh deh gohlf*
gone	perdido	*pehrdeedoh*
good afternoon	buenas tardes (after 2pm)	*bwehnahs tahrdehs*
good evening	buenas tardes	*bwehnahs tahrdehs*
good morning	buenos días (before 2pm)	*bwehnohs deeahs*
good night	buenas noches	*bwehnahs nohchehs*
goodbye	la despedida	*lah dehspehdeedah*
gram	el gramo	*ehl grahmoh*
grandchild	el nieto	*ehl nyehtoh*

grandfather	el abuelo	*ehl ahbwehloh*
grandmother	la abuela	*lah ahbwehlah*
grape juice	el zumo de uvas	*ehl thoomoh deh oobahs*
grapefruit	el pomelo	*ehl pohmehloh*
grapes	las uvas	*lahs oobahs*
grave	la tumba	*lah toombah*
grease	la grasa	*lah grahsah*
green	verde	*behrdeh*
green card	la tarjeta verde	*lah tahrhehtah behrdeh*
greet	saludar	*sahloodahr*
grey (hair)	canoso	*kahnohsoh*
grey	gris	*grees*
grill (verb)	asar a la parrilla	*ahsahr ah lah pahreelyah*
grilled	tostado	*tohstahdoh*
grocer's	la tienda de comestibles	*lah tyehndah deh kohmehsteeblehs*
ground	la tierra	*lah tyehrrah*
group	el grupo	*ehl groopoh*
guest house	la pensión	*lah pehnsyohn*
guide (book)	la guía	*lah gueeah*
guide (person)	el/la guía	*ehl/lah gueeah*
guided tour	la visita guiada	*lah beeseetah gueeahdah*
gynaecologist	el ginecólogo	*ehl heenehkohlohgoh*

H

hair	el pelo	*ehl pehloh*
hairbrush	el cepillo para el pelo	*ehl thehpeelyoh parah ehl pehloh*
hairdresser (ladies', men's)	la peluquería (de señoras, caballeros)	*lah pehlookehreeah (deh sehnyohrahs, kahbahlyehrohs)*
hairpins	las horquillas	*lahs ohrkeelyahs*
hairspray	la laca para el pelo	*lah lahkah pahrah ehl pehloh*
half	medio, media, la mitad	*mehdyoh, mehdyah, lah meetahdh*
half full	lleno hasta la mitad	*lyehnoh ahstah lah meetahdh*
half kilo	el medio kilo	*ehl mehdyoh keeloh*
hammer	el martillo	*ehl mahrteelyoh*
hand	la mano	*lah mahnoh*
hand brake	el freno de mano	*ehl frehnoh deh mahnoh*
handbag	el bolso de mano	*ehl bohlsoh deh mahnoh*
handbag	el bolso	*ehl bohlsoh*
handkerchief	el pañuelo	*ehl pahnywehloh*
handmade	hecho a mano	*ehchoh ah mahnoh*
happy	contento	*kohntehntoh*
harbour	el puerto	*ehl pwehrtoh*
hard	duro	*dooroh*
haste	la prisa	*lah preesah*
hat	el sombrero	*ehl sohmbrehroh*

hay fever	la fiebre del heno	*lah fyehbreh dehl ehnoh*
hazelnut	la avellana	*lah ahbehlyahnah*
head	la cabeza	*lah kahbehthah*
headache	el dolor de cabeza	*ehl dohlohr deh kahbehthah*
health	la salud	*lah sahloodh*
health food shop	la tienda naturista	*lah tyehndah nahtooreestah*
hear	entender	*ehntehndehr*
hearing aid	el audífono	*ehl ahoodeefohnoh*
heart	el corazón	*ehl kohrahthohn*
heart patient	el enfermo cardíaco	*ehl ehnfehrmoh kahrdeeahkoh*
heat	calor	*kahlohr*
heater	la calefacción	*lah kahlehfahkthyohn*
heavy	pesado	*pehsahdoh*
heel	el talón	*ehl tahlohn*
heel (on shoe)	el tacón	*ehl tahkohn*
hello	hola	*ohlah*
helmet	el casco	*ehl kahskoh*
help (verb)	ayudar	*ahyoodahr*
help	la ayuda	*lah ahyoodah*
helping/portion	la ración	*lah rahthyohn*
herbal tea	la infusión	*lah eenfoosyohn*
here	aquí	*ahkee*
herring	el arenque	*ehl ahrehnkeh*
high	alto	*ahltoh*
high tide	la marea alta	*lah mahrehah ahltah*
highchair	la silla para niños	*lah seelyah pahrah neenyohs*
hiking	el excursionismo	*ehl ehxkoorsyohneesmoh*
hiking trip	la excursión a pie	*lah ehxkoorsyohn ah pyeh*
hip	la cadera	*lah kahdehrah*
hire	alquilar	*ahlkeelahr*
hitchhike	hacer autostop	*ahthehr ahootohstohp*
hobby	el hobby	*ehl hohbee*
hold-up/robbery	el asalto	*ehl ahsahltoh*
holiday (public)	el día de fiesta	*ehl deeah deh fyehstah*
holiday house	el chalet	*ehl chahleh*
holiday park	la urbanización	*lah oorbahneethah-thyohn*
holidays	las vacaciones	*lahs bahkahthyohnehs*
home (at)	en casa	*ehn kahsah*
homesickness	la nostalgia	*lah nohstahl<u>h</u>yah*
honest	sincero	*seenthehroh*
honey	la miel	*lah myehl*
horizontal	horizontal	*oreethohntahl*
horrible	horrible	*ohrreebleh*
horse	el caballo	*ehl kahbahlyoh*
hospital	el hospital	*ehl ohspeetahl*
hospitality	la hospitalidad	*lah ohspeetahleedahdh*
hot	cálido/caluroso	*kahleedoh/ kahloorohsoh*
hot (spicy)	picante	*peekahnteh*

Word list

15

131

hotel	el hotel	*ehl ohtehl*
hot-water bottle	la bolsa de agua caliente	*lah bohlsah deh ahgwah kahlyehnteh*
hour	la hora	*lah ohrah*
house	la casa	*lah kahsah*
household items	los artículos del hogar	*lohs ahrteekoolohs dehl ohgahr*
houses of parliament	la cámara de diputados	*lah kahmahrah deh deepootahdohs*
housewife	el ama de casa	*ehl ahmah deh kahsah*
how far?	¿a qué distancia?	*ah keh deestahnthyah?*
how long?	¿cuánto tiempo?	*kwahntoh tyehmpoh?*
how much?	¿cuánto?	*kwahntoh?*
how?	¿cómo?	*kohmoh*
hunger	el hambre/el apetito	*ehl ahmbreh/ehl ahpehteetoh*
hurricane	el huracán	*ehl oorahkahn*
hurry	la prisa	*lah preesah*
husband	el marido	*ehl mahreedoh*
hut	el camarote	*ehl kahmahrohteh*
hyperventilation	la hiperventilación	*lah eepehr-behnteelahthyohn*

I

ice cream	el helado	*ehl ehlahdoh*
ice cubes	los cubitos de hielo	*lohs koobeetohs deh yehloh*
ice skating	el patinaje sobre hielo	*ehl pahteenahhheh sohbreh yehloh*
idea	la idea	*lah eedehah*
identification card	el carnet de identidad	*ehl kahrneh deh eedehnteedad*
identify	identificar	*eedehnteefeekahr*
ignition key	la llave de contacto	*lah lyahbeh deh kohntahktoh*
ill	enfermo	*ehnfehrmoh*
illness	la enfermedad	*lah ehnfehrmehdahdh*
imagine	imaginarse	*eemahhheenahrseh*
immediately	inmediatamente	*eenmehdyahtah-mehnteh*
import duty	los derechos de aduana	*lohs dehrehchohs deh ahdwahnah*
impossible	imposible	*eempohseebleh*
in	en	*ehn*
in the evening	por la tarde	*pohr lah tahrdeh*
in the morning	por la mañana	*pohr lah mahnyahnah*
included	incluido	*eenklooeedoh*
indicate	señalar	*sehnyahlahr*
indicator	el intermitente	*ehl eentehrmeetehnteh*
inexpensive	barato	*bahrahtoh*
infection (viral -, bacterial -)	la infección (vírica, bacteriana)	*lah eenfehkthyohn (beereekah, bahktehryahnah)*
inflammation	la inflamación	*lah eenflahmahthyohn*
information	la información	*lah eenfohrmahthyohn*
information office	la oficina de información	*lah ohfeetheenah deh eenfohrmahthyohn*

injection	la inyección	*lah eenyehkthyohn*
injured	herido	*erhreedoh*
inner ear	el oído	*ehl oheedoh*
inner tube	la cámara	*lah kahmahrah*
innocent	inocente	*eenohthehnteh*
insect	el insecto	*ehl eensehktoh*
insect bite	la picadura de insecto	*lah peekahdoorah deh eensehktoh*
insect repellant	el aceite para los mosquitos	*ehl ahthehyteh pahrah lohs mohskeetohs*
inside	adentro	*ahdehntroh*
insole	la plantilla	*lah plahnteelyah*
instructions	las instrucciones	*lahs eenstrookthyohnehs*
insurance	el seguro	*ehl sehgooroh*
intermission	la pausa	*lah pahoosah*
international	internacional	*eentehrnahthyohnahl*
interpreter	el intérprete	*ehl eentehrprehteh*
intersection/crossing	el cruce	*ehl krootheh*
introduce oneself	presentarse	*prehsehntahrseh*
invite (verb)	invitar	*eenbeetahr*
iodine	el yodo	*ehl yohdoh*
iron (metal)	el hierro	*ehl yehrroh*
iron (verb)	planchar	*plahnchahr*
iron	la plancha	*lah plahnchah*
ironing board	la tabla de planchar	*lah tahblah deh plahnchahr*
island	la isla	*lah eeslah*
it's a pleasure	de nada	*deh nahdah*
Italian	italiano	*eetahlyahnoh*
itch	la picazón	*lah peekahthohn*

J

jack	el gato	*ehl gahtoh*
jacket	la chaqueta	*lah chahkehtah*
jam	la mermelada	*lah mehrmehlahdah*
January	enero	*ehnehroh*
jaw	la mandíbula	*lah mahndeeboolah*
jellyfish	la medusa	*lah mehdoosah*
jeweller	la joyería	*lah hoyehreeah*
jewels	las alhajas	*lahs ahlahhahs*
jog (verb)	hacer footing	*ahthehr footeen*
joke	la broma	*lah brohmah*
journey	el viaje	*ehl byahheh*
juice	el zumo/el jugo	*ehl thoomoh/ehl hoogoh*
July	julio	*hoolyoh*
jump leads	el cable de arranque	*ehl kahbleh deh ahrrahnkeh*
jumper	el jersey	*ehl hehrsehee*
June	junio	*hoonyoh*

K

key	la llave	*lah lyahbeh*
kilo	el kilo	*ehl keeloh*
kilometre	kilómetro(s)	*keelohmehtroh(s)*
king	el rey	*ehl rehee*

kiss (verb)	besar	behsahr
kiss	el beso	ehl behsoh
kitchen	la cocina	lah kohteenah
knee	la rodilla	lah rohdeelyah
knee socks	las medias cortas	lahs mehdyahs kohrtahs
knife	el cuchillo	ehl koocheelyoh
know	saber	sahbehr

L

lace	el encaje	ehl ehnkah<u>h</u>eh
ladies'	el servicio para señoras	ehl sehrbeethyoh pahrah sehnyohrahs
lake	el lago	ehl lahgoh
lamp	la lámpara	lah lahmpahrah
land (verb)	aterrizar	ahtehrreethahr
lane	el carril	ehl kahrreel
language	el idioma	ehl eedyohmah
large	grande	grahndeh
last	pasado, último	pahsahdoh, oolteemoh
last night	anoche	ahnohcheh
late	tarde	tahrdeh
later	luego	lwehgoh
latest (at the)	a más tardar	ah mahs tahrdahr
laugh	reír	reheer
launderette	la lavandería (automática)	lah lahbahndehreeah (ahootohmahteekah)
law	el derecho	ehl dehrehchoh
laxative	el laxante	ehl lahxahnteh
leak	pinchado	peenchahdoh
leather	la piel, el cuero	lah pyehl, ehl kwehroh
leather goods	los artículos de piel	lohs ahrteekoolohs deh pyehl
leave (verb)	partir, salir	pahrteer, sahleer
leek	el puerro	ehl pwehrroh
left (on the)	a la izquierda	ah lah eethkyehrdah
left	izquierda	eethkyehrdah
left luggage	el depósito de equipajes	ehl dehpohseetoh deh ehkeepah<u>h</u>ehs
leg	la pierna	lah pyehrnah
lemon	el limón	ehl leemohn
lemonade	la limonada	lah leemohnahdah
lend	prestar	prehstahr
lens	el objetivo	ehl ohb<u>h</u>ehteeboh
lentils	las lentejas	lahs lehnteh<u>h</u>ahs
less	menos	mehnohs
lesson	la clase	lah klahseh
letter	la carta	lah kahrtah
lettuce	la lechuga	lah lehchoogah
level crossing	el paso a nivel	ehl pahsoh ah neebehl
library	la biblioteca	lah beeblyohtehkah
lie	mentir	mehnteer
lie down	estar tumbado	ehstahr toombahdoh
lift (hitchhike)	el viaje (en autostop)	ehl byah<u>h</u>eh (ehn ahootohstohp)
lift (in building)	el ascensor	ehl ahsthehnsohr

lift (ski)	el telesquí, el telesilla	*ehl tehlehskee, ehl*
		tehlehseelyah
light (for cigarette)	el fuego	*ehl fwehgoh*
light (not dark)	claro	*klahroh*
light (not heavy)	ligero	*leehehroh*
lighter	el mechero	*ehl mehchehroh*
lighthouse	el faro	*ehl fahroh*
lightning	el rayo	*ehl rahyoh*
like	gustar	*goostahr*
line	la línea	*lah leenehah*
linen	el hilo	*ehl eeloh*
lipstick	la barra de labios	*lah bahrrah deh*
		lahbyohs
liqueur	la copa	*lah kohpah*
liquorice	el regaliz	*ehl rehgahleeth*
listen	escuchar	*ehskoochahr*
literature	la literatura	*lah leetehrahtoorah*
litre	el litro	*ehl leetroh*
little	poco	*pohkoh*
live (verb)	vivir	*beebeer*
live together	vivir con otra	*beebeer kohn ohtrah*
	persona	*pehrsohnah*
lobster	la langosta	*lah lahngohstah*
local	local	*lohkahl*
lock	la cerradura	*lah thehrrahdoorah*
long	largo	*lahrgoh*
look (verb)	mirar	*meerahr*
look for	buscar	*booskahr*
look up (person)	buscar	*booskahr*
lorry	el camión	*ehl kahmyohn*
lose	perder	*pehrdehr*
loss	la pérdida	*lah pehrdeedah*
lost (to get)	perderse, extraviarse	*pehrdehrseh,*
		ehxtrahbyahrseh
lost	extraviado, perdido	*ehxtrahbyahdoh,*
		pehrdeedoh
lost item	extravío	*ehxtrahbeeoh*
lost property office	los objetos perdidos	*lohs ohbhehtohs*
		pehrdeedohs
lotion	la loción	*lah lohthyohn*
loud	alto	*ahltoh*
love (be in - with)	estar enamorado de	*ehstahr*
		ehnahmohrahdoh deh
love (verb)	querer	*kehrehr*
love	el amor	*ehl ahmohr*
low	bajo	*bahhoh*
low tide	la marea baja	*lah mahrehah bahhah*
luck	la suerte	*lah swehrteh*
luggage	el equipaje	*ehl ehkeepahheh*
luggage locker	la consigna	*lah kohnseegnah*
	automática	*ahootohmahteekah*
lunch	el almuerzo, la	*ehl ahlmwehrthoh,*
	comida	*lah kohmeedah*
lungs	los pulmones	*lohs poolmohnehs*

M

macaroni	los macarrones	*lohs mahkahrrohnehs*
madam/Mrs	señora	*sehnyohrah*
magazine	la revista	*lah rehbeestah*
magnificent	magnífico	*mahgneefeekoh*
mail	el correo	*ehl kohrrehoh*
main post office	la oficina central de Correos	*ah ohfeetheenah thehntrahl deh kohrrehohs*
main road	la carretera principal	*lah kahrrehtehrah preentheepahl*
make an appointment	pedir hora	*pehdeer ohrah*
make love	acostarse/hacer el amor	*ahkohstahrseh/ahthehr ehl ahmohr*
makeshift	provisional(mente)	*prohbeesyohnahl (mehnteh)*
man	el hombre	*ehl ohmbreh*
manager	el encargado	*ehl ehnkahrgahdoh*
mandarin	la mandarina	*lah mahndahreenah*
manicure	la manicura	*lah mahneekoorah*
map	el mapa	*ehl mahpah*
marble	el mármol	*ehl mahrmohl*
March	marzo	*mahrthoh*
margarine	la margarina	*lah mahrgahreenah*
marina	el puerto deportivo	*ehl pwehrtoh dehpohrteeboh*
market	el mercado	*ehl mehrkahdoh*
marriage	el matrimonio	*ehl mahtreemohnyoh*
married	casado	*kahsahdoh*
mass	la misa	*lah meesah*
massage	el masaje	*ehl mahsahheh*
mat	mate	*mahteh*
matches	las cerillas	*lahs thehreelyahs*
May	mayo	*mahyoh*
maybe	quizá	*keethah*
mayonnaise	la mayonesa	*lah mahyohnehsah*
mayor	el alcalde	*ehl ahlkahldeh*
meal	la comida	*lah kohmeedah*
mean (verb)	significar	*seegneefeekahr*
meat	la carne	*lah kahrneh*
medical insurance	el seguro de enfermedad	*ehl sehgooroh deh ehnfehrmehdahdh*
medication	el medicamento	*ehl mehdeekahmehntoh*
medicine	el medicamento, la medicina	*ehl mehdeekahmehntoh, lah mehdeetheenah*
meet	conocer	*kohnohthehr*
melon	el melón	*ehl mehlohn*
membership	el ser socio	*ehl sehr sohthyoh*
menstruate	tener la regla	*tehnehr lah rehglah*
menstruation	la menstruación	*lah mehnstrooahthyohn*
menu	el menú, la carta	*ehl mehnoo, lah kahrtah*
menu of the day	el menú del día	*ehl mehnoo dehl deeah*
message	el recado/mensaje	*ehl rehkahdoh/ mehnsahheh*

metal	el metal	*ehl mehtahl*
meter (taxi)	el taxímetro	*ehl tahxeemehtroh*
metre	metro(s)	*mehtroh(s)*
migraine	la jaqueca	*lah hahkehkah*
mild (tobacco)	rubio	*roobyoh*
milk	la leche	*lah lehcheh*
millimetre(s)	milímetro(s)	*meeleemehtroh(s)*
milometer	el cuentakilómetros	*ehl kwehntah-keelohmehtrohs*
mince	la carne picada	*lah kahrneh peekahdah*
mineral water	el agua mineral	*ehl ahgwah meenehrahl*
minute	el minuto	*ehl meenootoh*
mirror	el espejo	*ehl ehspehoh*
miss (person)	echar de menos	*ehchahr deh mehnohs*
missing (be)	faltar	*fahltahr*
mistake	el error, la equivocación	*ehl ehrrohr, lah ehkeebohkahthyohn*
mistaken (be)	equivocarse	*ehkeebohkahrseh*
misunderstanding	el malentendido	*ehl mahlehntehndeedoh*
mixture	el jarabe, la poción	*ehl hahrahbeh, lah pohthyohn*
mocha	el moca	*ehl mohkah*
modern art	el arte moderno	*ehl ahrteh mohdehrnoh*
molar	la muela	*lah mwehlah*
moment	el momento	*ehl mohmehntoh*
Monday	el lunes	*ehl loonehs*
money	el dinero	*ehl deenehroh*
month	el mes	*ehl mehs*
moped	el ciclomotor	*ehl theeklohmohtohr*
morning-after pill	la píldora para el día después	*lah peeldohrah pahrah ehl deeah dehspwehs*
mosque	la mezquita	*lah methkeetah*
motel	el motel	*ehl mohtehl*
mother	la madre	*lah mahdreh*
motor cross	el motocrós	*ehl mohtohkrohs*
motorbike	la moto	*lah mohtoh*
motorboat	la lancha motora	*lah lahnchah mohtohrah*
motorway	la autovía, la autopista	*lah ahootohbeeah, lah ahootohpeestah*
mountain	la montaña	*lah mohntahnyah*
mountain hut	el refugio	*ehl rehfoohyoh*
mountaineering	el montañismo	*ehl mohntahnyeesmoh*
mountaineering shoes	las botas de alpinismo	*lahs bohtahs deh ahlpeeneesmoh*
mouse	el ratón	*ehl rahtohn*
mouth	la boca	*lah bohkah*
much/many	mucho	*moochoh*
multi-storey car park	el estacionamiento	*ehl ehstahthyohnah-myehntoh*
muscle	el músculo	*ehl mooskooloh*
muscle spasms	los calambres (en los músculos)	*lohs kahlahmbrehs (ehn lohs mooskoolohs)*
museum	el museo	*ehl moosehoh*
mushrooms	las setas	*lahs sehtahs*
music	la música	*lah mooseekah*

Word list

15

musical show	la comedia musical	*lah kohmehdyah mooseekahl*
mussels	los mejillones	*lohs meheelyohnehs*
mustard	la mostaza	*lah mohstahthah*

N

nail (on hand)	la uña	*lah oonyah*
nail	el clavo	*ehl klahboh*
nail polish	el esmalte (para uñas)	*ehl ehsmahlteh(pahrah oonyahs)*
nail polish remover	el quitaesmalte	*ehl keetahehsmahlteh*
nail scissors	las tijeras de uñas	*lahs tee<u>h</u>ehrahs pahrah oonyahs*
naked	desnudo	*dehsnoodoh*
nappy	el pañal	*ehl pahnyahl*
nationality	la nacionalidad	*lah nahthyohnahlee-dahdh*
nature	la naturaleza	*lah nahtoorahlehthah*
naturism	el naturismo	*ehl nahtooreesmoh*
nauseous	con náuseas	*kohn nahoosehahs*
near	junto a	*<u>h</u>oontoh ah*
nearby	cerca	*thehrkah*
necessary	necesario	*nehthehsahryoh*
neck	la nuca	*lah nookah*
necklace	la cadena	*lah kahdehnah*
needle	la aguja	*lah ahoo<u>h</u>ah*
negative	el negativo	*ehl nehgahteeboh*
neighbours	los vecinos	*lohs behtheenohs*
nephew	el sobrino	*ehl sohbreenoh*
Netherlands	los Países Bajos	*lohs paheesehs bah<u>h</u>ohs*
never	jamás/nunca	*<u>h</u>ahmahs/noonkah*
new	nuevo	*nwehboh*
news	las noticias	*lahs nohteethyahs*
news stand	el quiosco	*ehl kyohskoh*
newspaper	el periódico	*ehl pehryohdeekoh*
next	próximo, que viene	*prohxeemoh, keh byehneh*
next to	al lado de	*ahl lahdoh deh*
nice (friendly)	amable	*ahmahbleh*
nice (to look at)	bonito, mono	*bohneetoh, mohnoh*
nice	bien, agradable	*byehn, ahgrahdahbleh*
niece	la sobrina	*lah sohbreenah*
night (at)	por la noche	*pohr lah nohcheh*
night	la noche	*lah nohcheh*
night duty	la guardia nocturna	*lah gwahrdyah nohktoornah*
nightclub	el cabaré	*ehl kahbahreh*
nightlife	la vida nocturna	*lah beedah nohktoornah*
nipple	la tetina	*lah tehteenah*
no	no	*noh*
no overtaking	la prohibición de adelantar	*lah proheebeethyohn deh ahdehlahntahr*
noise	el ruido	*ehl rooeedoh*
nonstop	sin escalas	*seen ehskahlahs*
no-one	nadie	*nahdyeh*

normal	normal, corriente	*nohrmahl, kohrryehnteh*
north	el norte	*ehl nohrteh*
nose	la nariz	*lah nahreeth*
nose bleed	la hemorragia nasal	*lah ehmohrrah<u>h</u>yah nahsahl*
nose drops	las gotas para la nariz	*lahs gohtahs pahrah lah nahreeth*
notepaper	el papel de escribir	*ehl pahpehl deh ehskreebeer*
nothing	nada	*nahdah*
November	noviembre	*nohbyehmbreh*
nowhere	en ninguna parte	*ehn neengoonah pahrteh*
nudist beach	la playa nudista	*lah plahyah noodeestah*
number	el número	*ehl noomehroh*
number plate	la matrícula	*lah mahtreekoolah*
nurse	la enfermera	*lah ehnfehrmehrah*
nutmeg	la nuez moscada	*lah nwehth mohskahdah*
nuts	los frutos secos	*lohs frootohs sehkohs*

O

October	octubre	*ohktoobreh*
of course	claro	*klahroh*
off	podrido	*pohdreedoh*
offer	ofrecer	*ohfrehthehr*
office	la oficina	*lah ohfeetheenah*
off-licence	la bodega, la tienda de vinos y licores	*lah bohdehgah, lah tyehndah deh beenohs ee leekohrehs*
oil	el aceite	*ehl ahtheyteh*
oil level	el nivel del aceite	*ehl neebehl deh ahtheyteh*
ointment	la pomada, el ungüento	*lah pohmahdah, ehl oongwehntoh*
ointment for burns	la pomada contra las quemaduras	*lah pohmahdah kohntrah lahs kehmahdoorahs*
okay	vale, de acuerdo	*bahleh, deh ahkwehrdoh*
old	viejo	*byeh<u>h</u>oh*
old part of town	el casco antiguo	*ehl kahskoh ahnteegwoh*
olive oil	el aceite de oliva	*ehl ahtheyteh deh ohleebah*
olives	las aceitunas	*lahs ahtheytoonahs*
omelette	la tortilla	*lah tohrteelyah*
on	sobre	*sohbreh*
on board	a bordo	*ah bohrdoh*
oncoming car	el vehículo que viene	*ehl beheekooloh keh byehneh*
one hundred grams	los cien gramos	*lohs thyehn grahmohs*
one-way traffic	la dirección única	*lah deerehkthyohn ooneekah*
onion	la cebolla	*lah thehbohlyah*
open (adj.)	abierto	*ahbyehrtoh*
open (verb)	abrir	*ahbreer*

Word list **15**

opera	la ópera	*lah ohpehrah*
operate	operar	*ohpehrahr*
operator (telephone)	la operadora	*lah ohpehrahdohrah*
operetta	la opereta, la zarzuela	*lah ohpehrehtah, lah thahrthwehlah*
opposite	al frente, enfrente de	*ahl frehnteh, ehnfrehnteh deh*
optician	la óptica	*lah ohpteekah*
orange	la naranja	*lah nahrahnhah*
orange (adj.)	naranja	*nahrahnhah*
orange juice	el zumo de naranja	*ehl thoomoh deh nahrahnhah*
order (in -,) tidy	en orden, ordenado	*ehn ohrdehn, ohrdehnahdo*
order (verb)	pedir	*pehdeer*
order	el pedido	*ehl pehdeedoh*
other	otro	*ohtroh*
other side	el otro lado	*ehl ohtroh lahdoh*
outside	afuera	*ahfwehrah*
overtake	adelantar	*ahdehlahntahr*
oysters	las ostras	*lahs ohstrahs*

P

packed lunch	el paquete con bocadillos	*ehl pahkehteh kohn bohkahdeelyohs*
page	la página	*lah pahheenah*
pain	el dolor	*ehl dohlohr*
painkiller	el analgésico	*ehl ahnahlhehseekoh*
paint (verb)	pintar	*peentahr*
paint	la pintura	*lah peentoorah*
painting (art)	el cuadro	*ehl kwahdroh*
painting (object)	la pintura	*lah peentoorah*
palace	el palacio	*ehl pahlahthyoh*
pancake	la crepe	*lah krehp*
pane	el cristal	*ehl kreestahl*
pants (briefs)	las bragas	*lahs brahgahs*
panty liner	el protegeslip	*ehl prohtehhehsleep*
paper	el papel	*ehl pahpehl*
paraffin oil	el querosén	*ehl kehrohsehn*
parasol	el quitasol	*ehl keetahsohl*
parcel	el paquete	*ehl pahkehteh*
pardon	perdone	*pehrdohneh*
parents	los padres	*lohs pahdrehs*
park	el parque	*ehl pahrkeh*
park (verb)	aparcar	*ahpahrkahr*
parking space	el sitio para aparcar	*ehl seetyoh pahrah ahpahrkahr*
parsley	el perejil	*ehl pehrehheel*
partition	la secreción	*lah sehkrehthyohn*
partner	la pareja	*lah pahrehhah*
party	la fiesta	*lah fyehstah*
passable	practicable	*prahkteekahbleh*
passenger	el pasajero	*ehl pahsahhehroh*
passport	el pasaporte	*ehl pahsahpohrteh*
passport photo	la foto de carnet	*lah fohtoh deh kahrneh*
patient	el paciente	*ehl pahthyehnteh*
pavement	la acera	*lah ahthehrah*

pay (verb)	pagar	*pahgahr*
pay the bill	pagar la cuenta	*pahgahr lah kwehntah*
peach	el melocotón	*ehl mehlohkohtohn*
peanuts	los cacahuetes	*lohs kahkahwehtehs*
pear	la pera	*lah pehrah*
peas	los guisantes	*lohs gueesahntehs*
pedal	el pedal	*ehl pehdahl*
pedestrian crossing	el paso de peatones	*ehl pahsoh deh pehahtohnehs*
pedicure	la pedicura	*lah pehdeekoorah*
pen	la pluma	*lah ploomah*
pencil (hard/soft)	el lápiz (duro/blando)	*ehl lahpeeth (dooroh /blahndoh)*
penis	el pene	*ehl pehneh*
pepper (capsicum)	el pimiento	*ehl peemyehntoh*
pepper (condiment)	la pimienta	*lah peemyehntah*
performance	la función de teatro /música	*lah foonthyohn deh tehahtroh/mooseekah*
perfume	el perfume	*ehl pehrfoomeh*
perm (verb)	hacer una permanente	*ahthehr oonah pehrmahnehnteh*
perm	la permanente	*lah pehrmahnehnteh*
permit	el permiso	*ehl pehrmeesoh*
person	la persona	*lah pehrsohnah*
personal	personal	*pehrsohnahl*
petrol	la gasolina	*lah gahsohleenah*
petrol station	la gasolinera	*lah gahsohleenehrah*
pets	los animales domésticos	*lohs ahneemahles dohmehsteekohs*
pharmacy	la farmacia	*lah fahrmahthyah*
phone (by)	por teléfono	*pohr tehlehfohnoh*
phone (tele-)	el teléfono	*ehl tehlehfohnoh*
phone (verb)	llamar por teléfono	*lyahmahr pohr tehlehfohnoh*
phone box	la cabina telefónica	*lah kahbeenah tehlehfohneekah*
phone directory	la guía de teléfonos	*lah gheeah deh tehlehfohnohs*
phone number	el número de teléfono	*ehl noomehroh deh tehlehfohnoh*
photo	la foto	*lah fohtoh*
photocopier	la fotocopiadora	*lah fohtohkohpyahdohrah*
photocopy (verb)	fotocopiar	*fohtohkohpyahr*
photocopy	la fotocopia	*lah fohtohkohpyah*
pick up (fetch person)	(ir a) buscar, pasar a buscar	*(eer ah) booskahr, pahsahr ah booskahr*
picnic	el picnic	*ehl peekneek*
piece of clothing	la prenda	*lah prehndah*
pier	el muelle	*ehl mwehlyeh*
pigeon	la paloma	*lah pahlohmah*
pill (contraceptive)	la píldora (anticonceptiva)	*lah peeldohrah (ahnteekohnthehp-teebah)*
pillow	la almohada	*lah ahlmohahdah*
pillowcase	la funda de almohada	*lah foondah deh ahlmohahdah*

pin	el alfiler	*ehl ahlfeelehr*
pineapple	la piña	*lah peenyah*
pipe	la pipa	*lah peepah*
pipe tobacco	el tabaco de pipa	*ehl tahbahkoh deh peepah*
pity	lástima	*lahsteemah*
place of entertainment	el sitio para salir	*ehl seetyoh pahrah sahleer*
place of interest	el punto de interés	*ehl poontoh deh eentehrehs*
plan/map	el plano	*ehl plahnoh*
plant	la planta	*lah plahntah*
plasters	las tiritas, los esparadrapos	*lahs teereetahs, lohs ehspahrah-drahpohs*
plastic	el plástico	*ehl plahsteekoh*
plastic bag	la bolsita	*lah bohlseetah*
plate	el plato	*ehl plahtoh*
platform	la vía, el andén	*lah beeah, ehl ahndehn*
play (theatre)	la obra de teatro	*lah ohbrah deh tehahtroh*
play (verb)	jugar	*hoogahr*
playground	el parque infantil	*ehl pahrkeh eenfahnteel*
playing cards	los naipes	*lohs naheepehs*
pleasant	agradable	*ahgrahdahbleh*
please	por favor	*pohr fahbohr*
pleasure	el placer	*ehl plahthehr*
plum	la ciruela	*lah theerwehlah*
pocketknife	la navaja	*lah nahbahhah*
point (verb)	indicar	*eendeekahr*
poison	el veneno	*ehl behnehnoh*
police	la policía	*lah pohleetheeah*
police station	la comisaría	*la kohmeesahreeah*
policeman	el guardia	*ehl gwahrdyah*
pond	el estanque	*ehl ehstahnkeh*
pony	el poney	*ehl pohnehy*
pop concert	el concierto pop	*ehl kohnthyehrtoh pohp*
population	la población	*lah pohblahthyohn*
pork	la carne de cerdo	*lah kahrneh deh thehrdoh*
port wine	el oporto	*ehl ohpohrtoh*
porter	el portero	*ehl pohrtehroh*
post code	el código postal	*ehl cohdeegoh pohstahl*
post office	la oficina de Correos	*lah ohfeetheenah deh cohrrehohs*
postage	el franqueo	*ehl frahnkehoh*
postbox	el buzón	*ehl boothohn*
postcard	la (tarjeta) postal	*lah (tahrhehtah) pohstahl*
postman	el cartero	*ehl kahrtehroh*
potato	la patata	*lah pahtahtah*
poultry	las aves	*lahs ahbehs*
powdered milk	la leche en polvo	*lah lehcheh ehn pohlboh*

power point	la toma de corriente	*lah tohmah deh kohrryehnteh*
pram	el cochecito	*ehl kohchehtheetoh*
prawns	las gambas	*lahs gahmbahs*
precious	querido	*kehreedoh*
prefer	preferir	*prehfehreer*
preference	la preferencia	*lah prehfehrehnthyah*
pregnant	embarazada	*ehmbahrahthahdah*
present	presente	*prehsehnteh*
present (gift)	el regalo	*ehl rehgahloh*
press (verb)	apretar	*ahprehtahr*
pressure	la tensión	*lah tehnsyohn*
price	el precio	*ehl prehthyoh*
price list	la lista de precios	*lah leestah deh prehthyohs*
print (verb)	copiar	*kohpyahr*
print	la copia	*lah kohpyah*
probably	probablemente	*prohbahblehmehnteh*
problem	el problema	*ehl prohblehmah*
profession	la profesión	*lah prohfehsyohn*
programme	el programa	*ehl prohgrahmah*
pronounce	pronunciar	*prohnoonthyahr*
propane camping gas	el gas propano	*ehl gahs prohpahnoh*
pull	sacar	*sahkahr*
pull a muscle	distender un músculo	*deestehndehr oon mooskooloh*
pure	puro	*pooroh*
purple	violeta	*beeohlehta*
purse	el monedero	*ehl mohnehdehroh*
push	empujar	*ehmpoo<u>h</u>ahr*
puzzle	el rompecabezas	*ehl rohmpehkahbehthahs*
pyjamas	el pijama	*ehl pee<u>h</u>ahmah*

Q

quarter	la cuarta parte	*lah kwahrtah pahrteh*
quarter of an hour	el cuarto de hora	*ehl kwahrtoh deh ohrah*
queen	la reina	*lah reheenah*
question	la pregunta	*lah prehgoontah*
quick	rápido	*rahpeedoh*
quiet	tranquilo	*trahnkeeloh*

R

radio	la radio	*lah rahdyoh*
railways	los ferrocarriles	*lohs fehrrohkahrreelehs*
rain (verb)	llover	*lyohbehr*
rain	la lluvia	*lah lyoobyah*
raincoat	el impermeable	*ehl eempehrmehahbleh*
raisins	las uvas pasas	*lahs oobahs pahsahs*
rape	la violación	*lah beeohlahthyohn*
rapids	el rápido	*ehl rahpeedoh*
rash (skin)	la erupción cutánea	*lah ehroopthyohn kootahnehah*
raspberries	las frambuesas	*lahs frahmbwehsahs*
raw	crudo	*kroodoh*
raw ham	el jamón (serrano)	*ehl <u>h</u>ahmohn sehrrahnoh*

raw vegetables	las verduras crudas	lahs behrdoorahs kroodahs
razor blades	las hojas de afeitar	lahs ohahs deh ahfeheetahr
read (verb)	leer	lehehr
ready	listo	leestoh
really	en realidad	ehn rehahleedahdh
receipt	el recibo	ehl rehtheeboh
recipe	la receta	lah rehthehtah
reclining chair	la tumbona	lah toombohnah
recommend	recomendar	rehkohmehndahr
rectangle	el rectángulo	ehl rehktahngooloh
red	rojo	rohhoh
red wine	el vino tinto	ehl beenoh teentoh
refrigerator	el refrigerador	ehl rehfreehehrahdohr
regards	recuerdos	rehkwehrdohs
region	la región	lah rehhyohn
registered	certificado	thehrteefeekahdoh
relatives	los parientes	lohs pahryehntehs
reliable	fiable/seguro	fyahbleh/sehgooroh
religion	la religión	lah rehleehyohn
rent out	alquilar	ahlkeelahr
repair (verb)	arreglar	ahrrehglahr
repairs	el arreglo	ehl ahrrehgloh
repeat	repetir	rehpehteer
report	el atestado	ehl ahtehstahdoh
resent	tomar a mal	tohmahr ah mahl
responsible	responsable	rehspohnsahbleh
rest (verb)	descansar	dehskahnsahr
restaurant	el restaurante	ehl rehstahoorahnteh
retired	jubilado	hoobeeladoh
retirement	la jubilación	lah hoobeelahthyohn
return (ticket)	el billete de ida y vuelta	ehl beelyehteh deh eedah ee bwehltah
reverse (vehicle)	dar marcha atrás	dahr mahrchah ahtrahs
rheumatism	el reuma	ehl rehoomah
rice	el arroz	ehl ahrrohth
ridiculous	tontería(s)	tohntehreeah(s)
riding (horseback)	montar a caballo	mohntahr ah kahbahlyoh
riding school	el picadero	ehl peekahdehroh
right	derecha	dehrehchah
right (on the)	a la derecha	ah lah dehrehchah
right of way	la preferencia	lah prehfehrehnthyah
ripe	maduro	mahdooroh
risk	el riesgo	ehl ryehsgoh
river	el río	ehl reeoh
road	el camino	ehl kahmeenoh
roadway	la calzada	lah kahlthahdah
roasted	asado	ahsahdoh
rock	la roca	lah rohkah
rolling tobacco	el tabaco para liar	ehl tahbahkoh pahrah leeahr
roof rack	la baca	lah bahkah
room	la habitación	lah ahbeetahthyohn
room number	el número de la habitación	ehl noomehroh deh lah ahbeetahthyohn

room service	el servicio en la habitación	*ehl sehrbeethyoh ehn lah ahbeetahthyohn*
rope	la cuerda	*lah kwehrdah*
rosé	el vino rosado	*ehl beenoh rohsahdoh*
roundabout	la rotonda	*lah rohtohndah*
route	la ruta	*lah rootah*
rowing boat	el bote de remos	*ehl bohteh deh rehmohs*
rubber	la goma	*lah gohmah*
rubbish	tontería(s)	*tohntehreeah(s)*
rucksack	la mochila	*lah mohcheelah*
rude	descortés/ maleducado	*dehskohrtehs/ mahlehdookahdoh*
ruins	las ruinas	*lahs rweenahs*
run into	encontrar	*ehnkohntrahr*

S

sad	triste	*treesteh*
safari	el safari	*ehl sahfahree*
safe	la caja fuerte	*lah kah<u>h</u>ah fwehrteh*
safe/secure	seguro	*sehgooroh*
safety pin	el imperdible	*ehl eempehrdeebleh*
sail	la vela	*lah behlah*
sailing boat	el velero	*ehl behlehroh*
salad	la ensalada	*lah ehnsahlahdah*
salad oil	el aceite	*ehl ahthehyteh*
salami	el salami	*ehl sahlahmee*
sale	las rebajas, la liquidación	*lahs rehbah<u>h</u>ahs, lah leekeedahthyohn*
salt	la sal	*lah sahl*
same	mismo	*meesmoh*
same	lo mismo	*loh meesmoh*
sandwich	el bocadillo	*ehl bohkahdeelyoh*
sandy beach	la playa de arena	*lah plahyah deh ahrehnah*
sanitary towel	la compresa	*lah kohmprehsah*
sardines	las sardinas	*lahs sahrdeenahs*
satisfied	contento	*kohntehntoh*
Saturday	el sábado	*ehl sahbahdoh*
sauce	la salsa	*lah sahlsah*
saucepan	la cacerola	*lah kahthehrohlah*
sauna	la sauna	*lah sahoonah*
sausage	el embutido	*ehl ehmbooteedoh*
savoury	salado	*sahlahdoh*
say (verb)	decir	*dehtheer*
scarf	la bufanda (woollen)	*lah boofahndah*
scarf	el pañuelo	*ehl pahnywehloh*
scenic walk	la visita a la ciudad (a pie)	*lah beeseetah ah lah thyoodahdh (ah pyeh)*
school	la escuela	*lah ehskwehlah*
scissors	las tijeras	*lahs tee<u>h</u>ehrahs*
scooter	la vespa	*lah behspah*
scorpion	el escorpión	*ehl ehskohrpyohn*
scrambled eggs	los huevos revueltos	*lohs wehbohs rehbwehltohs*
screw	el tornillo	*ehl tohrneelyoh*

Word list

15

screwdriver	el destornillador	*ehl dehstohrneelyahdohr*
sculpture	la escultura	*lah ehskooltoorah*
sea	el mar	*ehl mahr*
seasick	mareado	*mahrehahdoh*
seat	el asiento	*ehl ahsyehntoh*
seat	el asiento, la butaca	*ehl ahsyehntoh, lah bootahkah*
second (adj.)	segundo	*sehgoondoh*
second	el segundo	*ehl sehgoondoh*
second-hand	de segunda mano	*deh sehgoondah mahnoh*
sedative	el calmante	*ehl kahlmahnteh*
see (person)	visitar	*beeseetahr*
see	mirar	*meerahr*
self-timer	el disparador automático	*ehl deespahrahdohr ahootohmahteekoh*
semi-skimmed	semidesnatado	*sehmeedehsnahtahdoh*
send	enviar	*ehnbyahr*
sentence	la frase	*lah frahseh*
September	septiembre	*sehptyehmbreh*
serious	grave	*grahbeh*
service	el servicio	*ehl sehrbeethyoh*
serviette	la servilleta	*lah sehrbeelyehtah*
set (verb)	marcar	*mahrkahr*
sewing thread	el hilo de coser	*ehl eeloh deh kohsehr*
shade	la sombra	*lah sohmbrah*
shallow	poco profundo	*pohkoh prohfoondoh*
shampoo	el champú	*ehl chahmpoo*
shark	el tiburón	*ehl teeboorohn*
shave (verb)	afeitar	*ahfeheetahr*
shaver	la afeitadora eléctrica	*lah ahfehytahdohrah ehlehktreekah*
shaving brush	la brocha de afeitar	*lah brohchah deh ahfeheetahr*
shaving cream	la crema de afeitar	*lah krehmah deh ahfeheetahr*
shaving soap	el jabón de afeitar	*ehl <u>h</u>ahbohn deh ahfeheetahr*
sheet	la sábana	*lah sahbahnah*
sherry	el jerez	*ehl <u>h</u>ehrehth*
shirt	la camisa	*lah kahmeesah*
shoe	el zapato	*ehl thahpahtoh*
shoe polish	la crema de zapatos	*lah krehmah deh thahpahtohs*
shoe shop	la zapatería	*lah thahpahtehreeah*
shoelaces	los cordones	*lohs kohrdohnehs*
shoemaker	el zapatero	*ehl thahpahtehroh*
shop (verb)	hacer la compra	*ahthehr lah kohmprah*
shop	la tienda	*lah tyehndah*
shop assistant	la vendedora	*lah behndehdohrah*
shop window	el escaparate	*ehl ehskahpahrahteh*
shopping centre	el centro comercial	*ehl thehntroh kohmehrthyahl*
short	corto	*kohrtoh*
short circuit	el cortocircuito	*ehl kohrtohtheer-kweetoh*

Word list

15

shoulder	el hombro	*ehl ohmbroh*
show	el espectáculo	*ehl ehspehktahkooloh*
shower	la ducha	*lah doochah*
shutter	el obturador	*ehl ohbtoorahdohr*
sieve	el tamiz	*ehl tahmeeth*
sign (verb)	firmar	*feermahr*
sign	el cartel	*ehl kahrtehl*
signature	la firma	*lah feermah*
signposted walk	la excursión	*lah ehxkooresyohn*
	señalizada	*sehnyahleethahdah*
silence	el silencio	*ehl seelehnthyoh*
silver	la plata	*lah plahtah*
silver-plated	plateado	*plahtehahdoh*
simple	sencillo	*sehntheelyoh*
single (unmarried)	soltero	*sohltehroh*
single	individual	*eendeebeedwahl*
single ticket	el billete de ida	*ehl beelyehteh deh eedah*
sir	señor	*sehnyohr*
sister	la hermana	*lah ehrmahnah*
sit	estar sentado	*ehstahr sehntahdoh*
size (shoes)	el número	*ehl noomehroh*
size	la talla	*lah tahlyah*
ski boots	las botas de esquí	*lahs bohtahs deh ehskee*
ski goggles	las gafas de esquí	*lahs gahfahs deh ehskee*
ski instructor	el profesor de esquí	*ehl prohfehsohr deh ehskee*
ski lessons/class	la clase de esquiar	*lah klahseh deh ehskeeahr*
ski lift	el telesquí	*ehl tehlehskee*
ski pants	los pantalones de esquiar	*lohs pahntahlohnehs deh ehskeeahr*
ski pass	el bono (de remontes/ esquí)	*ehl bohnoh (deh rehmohntehs/ehskee)*
ski slope	la pista de esquí (alpino)	*lah peestah deh ehskee (ahlpeenoh)*
ski stick	el bastón de esquí	*ehl bahstohn deh ehskee*
ski suit	el traje de esquiar	*ehl trahheh deh ehskeeahr*
ski wax	la cera para esquí	*lah thehrah pahrah ehskee*
ski/skiing	esquiar, el esquí	*ehskeeahr, ehl ehskee*
skin	la piel	*lah pyehl*
skirt	la falda	*lah fahldah*
skis	los esquís	*lohs ehskees*
sleep (verb)	dormir	*dohrmeer*
sleep well!	que descanse	*keh dehskahnseh*
sleeping car	el coche cama	*ehl kohcheh kahmah*
sleeping pills	los somníferos	*lohs sohmneefehrohs*
slide	la diapositiva	*lah deeahpohseeteebah*
slip (women's)	la combinación	*lah kohmbeenahthyohn*
slip road	la entrada	*lah ehntrahdah*
slow	despacio	*dehspahthyoh*
slow train	el tren ómnibus	*ehl trehn ohmneeboos*

small	pequeño	*pehkehnyoh*
small change	el cambio, el dinero suelto	*ehl kahmbyoh, ehl deenehroh swehltoh*
smell unpleasant (verb)	oler mal	*ohlehr mahl*
smoke	el humo	*ehl oomoh*
smoke (verb)	fumar	*foomahr*
smoked	ahumado	*ahoomahdoh*
smoking compartment	el departamento de fumadores	*ehl dehpahrtahmehntoh deh foomahdohrehs*
snake	la serpiente	*lah sehrpyehnteh*
snorkel	el esnórquel	*ehl ehsnohrkehl*
snow (verb)	nevar	*nehbahr*
snow	la nieve	*lah nyehbeh*
snow chains	la cadena antideslizante	*lah kahdehnah ahnteedehsleethahnte*
soap	el jabón	*ehl hahbohn*
soap box	la jabonera	*lah hahbohnehrah*
soap powder	el jabón en polvo	*ehl hahbohn ehn pohlboh*
soccer	el fútbol	*ehl footbohl*
soccer match	el partido de fútbol	*ehl pahrteedoh deh footbohl*
socket	el enchufe	*ehl ehnchoofeh*
socks	los calcetines	*lohs kahlthehteenehs*
soft drink	el refresco	*ehl rehfrehskoh*
sole (fish)	el lenguado	*ehl lehngwahdoh*
sole	la suela	*lah swehlah*
solicitor	el abogado	*ehl ahbohgahdoh*
someone	alguien	*ahlguyehn*
sometimes	a veces	*ah behthehs*
somewhere	en alguna parte	*ehn ahlgoonah pahrteh*
son	el hijo	*ehl eehoh*
soon	pronto	*prohntoh*
sorbet	el sorbete	*ehl sohrbehteh*
sore	la úlcera	*lah oolthehrah*
sore throat	el dolor de garganta	*ehl dohlohr deh gahrgahntah*
sorry	perdón	*pehrdohn*
sort/type	la clase	*lah klahseh*
soup	la sopa	*lah sohpah*
sour	agrio	*ahgreeoh*
sour cream	la nata ácida	*lah nahtah ahtheedah*
source	la fuente	*lah fwehnteh*
south	el sur	*ehl soor*
souvenir	el recuerdo de viaje	*ehl rehkwehrdoh deh byahheh*
spaghetti	los espaguetis	*lohs ehspahgehtees*
Spanish	español	*ehspahnyohl*
spanner (openended)	la llave (de boca)	*lah lyahbeh(deh bohkah)*
spanner	la llave de tuercas	*lah lyahbeh deh twehrkahs*
spare	la reserva	*lah rehsehrbah*
spare part	la pieza de recambio	*lah pyehthah deh rehkahmbyoh*
spare tyre	el neumático de reserva	*ehl nehoomahteekoh deh rehsehrbah*

spare wheel	la rueda de recambio	*lah rwehdah deh rehkahmbyoh*
speak	hablar	*ahblahr*
special	especial	*ehspehthyahl*
specialist	el especialista	*ehl ehspethyahleestah*
specialty	la especialidad	*lah ehspehthyahleedah*
speed limit	la velocidad máxima	*lah behlohtheedah mahxeemah*
spell (verb)	deletrear	*dehlehtrehahr*
spicy	picante	*peekahnteh*
splinter	la astilla	*lah ahsteelyah*
spoon	la cuchara	*lah koochahrah*
spoonful	la cucharada	*lah koochahrahdah*
sport (play)	hacer deporte	*ahthehr dehpohrteh*
sport	el deporte	*ehl dehpohrteh*
sports centre	la sala de deportes	*lah sahlah deh dehpohrtehs*
spot/place	el sitio	*ehl seetyoh*
sprain (verb)	torcerse	*tohrthehrseh*
spring	la primavera	*lah preemahbehrah*
square	el cuadrado	*ehl kwahdrahdoh*
square (town)	la plaza	*lah plahthah*
square metre(s)	metro(s) cuadrado(s)	*mehtroh(s) kwahdrahdoh(s)*
squash	el squash	*ehl skwahsh*
stadium	el estadio	*ehl ehstahdyoh*
stain	la mancha	*lah mahnchah*
stain remover	el quitamanchas	*ehl keetahmahnchahs*
stairs	las escaleras	*lahs ehskahlehrahs*
stalls (theatre)	la platea	*lah plahtehah*
stamp	el sello	*ehl sehlyoh*
start (car)	arrancar	*ahrrahnkahr*
station	la estación	*lah ehstahthyohn*
statue	la estatua	*lah ehstahtooah*
stay (lodge)	alojarse	*ahlohhahrseh*
stay (verb)	quedarse	*kehdahrseh*
stay	la estancia	*lah ehstahnthyah*
steal (verb)	robar	*rohbahr*
steel, stainless	el acero, inoxidable	*ehl ahthehroh, eenohxeedahbleh*
stench	el mal olor	*ehl mahl ohlohr*
sting (verb)	picar	*peekahr*
stitch (med.)	el punto	*ehl poontoh*
stitch (verb)	suturar	*sootoorahr*
stock	el caldo	*ehl kahldoh*
stockings	las medias	*lahs mehdyahs*
stomach	el estómago, el vientre	*ehl ehstohmahgoh, ehl byehntreh*
stomach ache	el dolor de vientre/ estómago	*ehl dohlohr deh byehntreh/ ehstohmahgoh*
stomach cramps	los retortijones	*lohs rehtohrteehohnehs*
stools	las heces	*lahs ehthehs*
stop (verb)	parar	*pahrahr*
stop	la parada	*lah pahrahdah*
stopover	la escala	*lah ehskahlah*
storm	la tormenta	*lah tohrmehntah*

straight	liso	*leesoh*
straight ahead	todo recto	*tohdoh rehktoh*
straw	la pajita	*lah pah<u>h</u>eetah*
strawberries	las fresas	*lahs frehsahs*
street	la calle	*lah kahlyeh*
street side	el lado de la calle	*ehl lahdoh deh lah kahlyeh*
strike	la huelga	*lah wehlgah*
strong (tobacco)	negro	*nehgroh*
study (verb)	estudiar	*ehstoodyahr*
stuffing	el relleno	*ehl rehlyehnoh*
subscriber's number	el número de abonado	*ehl noomehroh deh ahbohnahdoh*
subtitled	subtitulada	*soobteetoolahdah*
succeed	salir bien	*sahleer byehn*
sugar	el azúcar	*ehl ahthookahr*
sugar lumps	los terrones de azúcar	*lohs tehrrohnehs deh ahthookahr*
suit	el traje	*ehl trah<u>h</u>eh*
suitcase	la maleta	*lah mahlehtah*
summer	el verano	*ehl behrahnoh*
summertime	la hora de verano	*lah ohrah deh behrahnoh*
sun	el sol	*ehl sohl*
sun hat	el sombrero de playa	*ehl sohmbrehroh deh plahyah*
sunbathe	tomar el sol	*tohmahr ehl sohl*
Sunday	el domingo	*ehl dohmeengoh*
sunglasses	las gafas de sol	*lahs gahfahs deh sohl*
sunrise	la salida del sol	*lah sahleedah dehl sohl*
sunset	la puesta del sol	*lah pwehstah dehl sohl*
sunstroke	la insolación	*lah eensohlahthyohn*
suntan lotion	la crema solar	*lah krehmah sohlahr*
suntan oil	el aceite bronceador	*ehl ahthehyteh brohnthehahdohr*
supermarket	el supermercado	*ehl soopehrmehrkahdoh*
surcharge	el suplemento	*ehl sooplehmehntoh*
surf	el surf	*ehl soorf*
surf board	la tabla de surf	*lah tahblah deh soorf*
surgery	la consulta	*lah kohnsooltah*
surname	el apellido	*ehl ahpehlyeedoh*
surprise	la sorpresa	*lah sohrprehsah*
swallow (verb)	tragar	*trahgahr*
swamp	el terreno pantanoso	*ehl tehrrehnoh pahntahnohsoh*
sweat	el sudor	*ehl soodohr*
sweet	el caramelo	*ehl kahrahmehloh*
sweet	dulce	*doolteh*
sweetcorn	el maíz	*ehl maheeth*
sweetener	la sacarina	*lah sahkahreenah*
sweets	las golosinas	*lahs gohlohseenahs*
swim (verb)	nadar	*nahdahr*
swimming pool	la piscina	*lah peestheenah*
swimming trunks	el bañador	*ehl bahnyahdohr*
swindle	la estafa	*lah ehstahfah*
switch	el interruptor	*ehl eentehrrooptohr*

synagogue	la sinagoga	lah seenahgohgah

T

table	la mesa	lah mehsah
table tennis	el pingpong	ehl peenpohn
tablet	la tableta	lah tahblehtah
take (photograph)	sacar	sahkahr
take (time)	durar, tardar	doorahr, tahrdahr
take (verb)	emplear, usar, tomar	ehmplehahr, oosahr, tohmahr
take pictures	fotografiar, sacar fotos	fohtohgrahfyahr, sahkahr fohtohs
taken	ocupado	ohkoopahdoh
talcum powder	el talco	ehl tahlkoh
talk (verb)	hablar	ahblahr
tampons	los tampones	lohs tahmpohnehs
tap	el grifo	ehl greefoh
tap water	el agua del grifo	ehl ahgwah dehl greefoh
tart	la tarta	lah tahrtah
taste (verb)	probar	prohbahr
tax free shop	la tienda libre de impuestos	lah tyehndah leebreh deh eempwehstohs
taxi	el taxi	ehl tahxee
taxi stand	la parada de taxis	lah pahrahdah deh tahxees
tea	el té	ehl teh
teapot	la tetera	lah tehtehrah
teaspoon	la cuchara de té	lah koochahrah deh teh
telegram	el telegrama	ehl tehlehgrahmah
telephoto lens	el teleobjetivo	ehl tehlehohbhehteeboh
television	la televisión	lah tehlehbeesyohn
telex	el télex	ehl tehlehx
temperature	la temperatura	lah tehmpehrahtoorah
temporary filling	el empaste provisional	ehl ehmpahsteh prohbeesyohnahl
tender	tierno	tyehrnoh
tennis	el tenis	ehl tehnees
tennis ball	la pelota de tenis	lah pehlohtah deh tehnees
tennis court	la pista de tenis	lah peestah deh tehnees
tennis racket	la raqueta de tenis	lah rahkehtah deh tehnees
tennis shoes	los zapatos de tenis	lohs thahpahtohs deh tehnees
tenpin bowling	los bolos	lohs bohlohs
tent	la tienda	lah tyehndah
tent peg	la estaca	lah ehstahkah
terrace	la terraza	lah tehrrahthah
terrible	terrible	tehrreebleh
thank (verb)	agradecer	ahgrahdehthehr
thank you	gracias	grahthyahs
thaw	deshelar	dehsehlahr
the day after tomorrow	pasado mañana	pahsahdoh mahnyahnah

Word list

15

theatre	el teatro	*ehl tehahtroh*
theft	el robo	*ehl rohboh*
there	allí	*ahlyee*
thermal bath	el baño termal	*ehl bahnyoh tehrmahl*
thermometer	el termómetro	*ehl tehrmohmehtroh*
thick	grueso/gordo	*grwehsoh/gohrdoh*
thief	el ladrón	*ehl lahdrohn*
thigh	el muslo	*ehl moosloh*
thin	fino, flaco	*feenoh, flahkoh*
things	las cosas	*lahs kohsahs*
think	pensar	*pehnsahr*
third	la tercera parte	*lah tehrthehrah pahrteh*
thirsty, to be	la sed	*lah sehdh*
this afternoon	esta tarde	*ehstah tahrdeh*
this evening	esta noche	*ehstah nohcheh*
this morning	esta mañana	*ehstah mahnyahnah*
thread	el hilo	*ehl eeloh*
throat	la garganta	*lah gahrgahntah*
throat lozenges	las pastillas para la garganta	*lahs pahsteelyahs pahrah lah gahrgahntah*
throw up	vomitar	*bohmeetahr*
thunderstorm	la tormenta eléctrica	*lah tohrmehntah ehlehktreekah*
Thursday	el jueves	*ehl hwehbehs*
ticket (admission)	la entrada	*lah ehntrahdah*
ticket (travel)	el billete	*ehl beelyehteh*
tickets	los billetes	*lohs beelyehtehs*
tidy (verb)	recoger	*rehkohehr*
tie	la corbata	*lah kohrbahtah*
tights	el leotardo, el panty	*ehl lehohtahrdoh, ehl pahntee*
time (occasion)	la vez	*lah behth*
time	el tiempo	*ehl tyehmpoh*
timetable	el horario	*ehl ohrahryoh*
tin	la lata	*lah lahtah*
tip (money)	la propina	*lah prohpeenah*
tissues	los pañuelitos de papel	*lohs pahnywehleetohs de pahpehl*
toast	el pan tostado, las tostadas	*ehl pahn tohstahdoh, lahs tohstahdahs*
tobacco	el tabaco	*ehl tahbahkoh*
toboggan	el trineo	*ehl treenehoh*
today	hoy	*ohee*
toe	el dedo del pie	*ehl dehdoh dehl pyeh*
together	juntos	*hoontohs*
toilet	el water/los servicios/ el lavabo	*ehl bahtehr/lohs sehrbeethyohs, ehl lahbahboh*
toilet paper	el papel higiénico	*ehl pahpehl eehyehneekoh*
toiletries	los artículos de tocador	*lohs ahrteekoolohs deh tohkahdohr*
tomato	el tomate	*ehl tohmahteh*
tomato purée	el tomate triturado	*ehl tohmahteh treetoorahdoh*
tomato sauce	el ketchup	*ehl kehchoop*
tomorrow	mañana	*mahnyahnah*

tongue	la lengua	*lah lehngwah*
tonic water	el agua tónica	*ehl agwah tohneekah*
tonight	esta noche	*ehstah nohcheh*
too much	demasiado	*dehmahsyahdoh*
tools	las herramientas	*lahs ehrrahmyehntahs*
tooth	el diente	*ehl dyehnteh*
toothache	el dolor de muelas	*ehl dohlohr deh mwehlahs*
toothbrush	el cepillo de dientes	*ehl thehpeelyoh deh dyehntehs*
toothpaste	el dentífrico	*ehl dehnteefreekoh*
toothpick	el palillo	*ehl pahleelyoh*
top up	rellenar	*rehlyehnahr*
total	el total	*ehl tohtahl*
tough	duro	*dooroh*
tour	la excursión, el paseo	*lah ehxkoorsyohn, ehl pahsehoh*
tour guide	el guía	*ehl gheeah*
tourist card	la tarjeta de turista	*lah tahr<u>h</u>ehtah deh tooreestah*
tourist class	la clase turista	*lah klahseh tooreestah*
Tourist Information office	la oficina de (información y) turismo	*lah ohfeetheenah deh (eenfohrmahthyohn ee) tooreesmoh*
tourist menu	el menú turístico	*ehl mehnoo tooreesteekoh*
tow	remolcar	*rehmohlkahr*
tow cable	el cable de remolque	*ehl kahbleh deh rehmohlkeh*
towel	la toalla	*lah tohahlyah*
tower	la torre	*lah tohrreh*
town hall	el ayuntamiento	*ehl ahyoontahmyehntoh*
town/city	la ciudad	*lah thyoodahdh*
toys	los juguetes	*lohs hooguehtehs*
traffic	el tráfico	*ehl trahfeekoh*
traffic light	el semáforo	*ehl sehmahfohroh*
trailer tent	el remolque tienda	*ehl rehmohlkeh tyehndah*
train	el tren	*ehl trehn*
train ticket	el billete de tren	*ehl beelyehteh deh trehn*
train timetable	la guía de trenes	*lah gueeah deh trehnehs*
translate	traducir	*trahdootheer*
travel (verb)	viajar	*byah<u>h</u>ahr*
travel agent	la agencia de viajes	*lah ah<u>h</u>ehnthyah deh byah<u>h</u>ehs*
travel guide	la guía	*lah gheeah*
traveller	el pasajero	*ehl pahsah<u>h</u>ehroh*
traveller's cheque	el cheque de viajero	*ehl chehkeh deh byah<u>h</u>ehroh*
treacle/syrup	la melaza	*lah mehlahthah*
treatment	el tratamiento	*ehl trahtahmyehntoh*
triangle	el triángulo	*ehl treeahngooloh*
trim	cortar las puntas	*kohrtahr lahs poontahs*

trip	el paseo, la excursión	*ehl pahsehoh,lah ehxkoorsyohn*
trouble	la molestia	*lah mohlehstyah*
trousers (long, short)	los pantalones (cortos, largos)	*lohs pahntahlohnehs (kohrtohs,lahrgohs)*
trout	la trucha	*lah troochah*
trunk call	interurbano	*eentehroorbahnoh*
trunk code	el prefijo	*ehl prehfeehoh*
trustworthy	digno de confianza	*deegnoh deh kohnfyahnthah*
try on (clothes)	probarse	*prohbahrseh*
T-shirt	la camiseta	*lah kahmeesehtah*
tube	el tubo	*ehl tooboh*
Tuesday	el martes	*ehl mahrtehs*
tumble drier	la secadora	*lah sehkahdohrah*
tuna	el atún	*ehl ahtoon*
tunnel	el túnel	*ehl toonehl*
turn	la vez	*lah behth*
TV	la televisión	*lah tehlehbeesyohn*
tv and radio guide	la guía de radio y televisión	*lah gheeah deh rahdyoh ee tehlehbeesyohn*
tweezers	los alicates	*lohs ahleekahtehs*
tyre (bicycle)	la cubierta	*lah koobyehrtah*
tyre lever	el desmontador de neumáticos	*ehl dehsmohntahdohr deh nehoomahteekohs*
tyre pressure	la presión de los neumáticos	*lah prehsyohn deh lohs nehoomahteekohs*

U

ugly	feo	*fehoh*
umbrella	el paraguas	*ehl pahrahgwahs*
under	abajo, debajo de	*ahbah<u>h</u>oh, dehbah<u>h</u>oh deh*
underground railway	el metro	*ehl mehtroh*
underground railway system	la red de metro	*lah rehdh deh mehtroh*
underground station	la estación de metro	*lah ehstahthyohn deh mehtroh*
underpants	los calzoncillos	*lohs kahlthohntheelyohs*
understand	entender	*ehntehndehr*
underwear	la ropa interior	*lah rohpah eentehryohr*
undress (verb)	desvestirse	*dehsbehsteerseh*
unemployed	en paro	*ehn pahroh*
uneven	desigual	*dehseegwahl*
university	la universidad	*lah ooneebehrseedah*
unleaded	sin plomo	*seen plohmoh*
urgent	urgente	*oor<u>h</u>ehnteh*
urine	la orina	*lah ohreenah*
usually	por lo general	*pohr loh <u>h</u>ehnehrahl*

V

vacate	desalojar	*dehsahloh<u>h</u>ahr*
vaccinate	vacunarse	*bahkoonahrseh*
vagina	la vagina	*lah bah<u>h</u>eenah*
vaginal infection	la infección vaginal	*lah eenfehkthyohn bah<u>h</u>eenal*

valid	válido	*bahleedoh*
valley	el valle	*ehl bahlyeh*
valuable	costoso	*kohstohsoh*
van	la furgoneta	*lah foorgohnehtah*
vanilla	la vainilla	*lah baheeneelyah*
vase	el florero	*ehl flohrehroh*
vaseline	la vaselina	*lah bahsehleenah*
veal	la carne de ternera	*lah kahrneh deh tehrnehrah*
vegetable soup	la sopa de verduras	*lah sohpah deh behrdoorahs*
vegetables	la verdura	*lah behrdoorah*
vegetarian	vegetariano	*beh<u>h</u>ehtahryahnoh*
vein	la vena	*lah vehnah*
vending machine	la máquina automática	*lah mahkeenah ahootohmahteekah*
venereal disease	la enfermedad venérea	*lah ehnfehrmehdah behnehrehah*
via	pasando por	*pahsahndoh pohr*
video recorder	el video	*ehl beedehoh*
video tape	la cinta de vídeo	*lah theentah deh beedehoh*
view	la vista	*lah beestah*
village	el pueblo	*ehl pwehbloh*
visa	el visado	*ehl beesahdoh*
visit (verb)	visitar	*beeseetahr*
visit	la visita	*lah beeseetah*
vitamin tablets	las tabletas de vitaminas	*lahs tahblehtahs deh beetahmeenahs*
vitamins	la vitamina	*lah beetahmeenah*
volcano	el volcán	*ehl bohlkahn*
volleyball (play)	jugar al vóleibol	*<u>h</u>oogahr ahl bohleheebohl*
vomit (verb)	vomitar	*bohmeetahr*

W

wait (verb)	esperar	*ehspehrahr*
waiter	el camarero	*ehl kahmahrehroh*
waiting room	la sala de espera	*lah sahlah deh ehspehrah*
waitress	la camarera	*lah kahmahrehrah*
wake up (verb)	despertar	*dehspehrtahr*
walk	el paseo	*ehl pahsehoh*
walk (take a)	salir a caminar	*sahleer ah kahmeenahr*
walk (verb)	ir (andando)	*eer(ahndahndoh)*
wallet	la cartera	*lah kahrtehrah*
wardrobe	el guardarropa	*ehl gwahrdahrrohpah*
warm	caliente	*kahlyehnteh*
warn	avisar, llamar	*ahbeesahr,lyahmahr*
warning	el aviso	*ehl ahbeesoh*
wash (verb)	lavar	*lahbahr*
washing (dirty)	la ropa sucia	*lah rohpah soothyah*
washing line	la cuerda de colgar la ropa	*lah kwehrdah deh kohlgahr lah rohpah*
washing machine	la lavadora	*lah lahbahdohrah*
washing-powder	el detergente	*ehl dehtehr<u>h</u>ehnteh*
wasp	la avispa	*lah ahbeespah*

Word list

15

watch	el reloj	*ehl rehlohh*
water	el agua	*ehl ahgwah*
water ski	el esquí acuático	*ehl ehskee ahkwahteekoh*
waterproof	impermeable	*eempehrmehahbleh*
wave-pool	la piscina con oleaje	*lah peestheenah kohn ohlehahheh*
way (means)	el remedio	*ehl rehmehdyoh*
way (on the)	en el camino	*ehn ehl kahmeenoh*
way	el lado	*ehl lahdoh*
we	nosotros	*nohsohtrohs*
weak	débil	*dehbeel*
weather	el tiempo	*ehl tyehmpoh*
weather forecast	el pronóstico del tiempo	*ehl prohnohsteekoh dehl tyehmpoh*
wedding	la boda	*lah bohdah*
Wednesday	el miércoles	*ehl myehrkohlehs*
week	la semana	*lah sehmahnah*
weekend	el fin de semana	*ehl feen deh sehmahnah*
weekend duty	la guardia de fin de semana	*lah gwahrdyah deh feen deh sehmahnah*
weekly ticket	el abono semanal	*ehl ahbohnoh sehmahnahl*
welcome	bienvenido	*byehnbehneedoh*
well	bien, bueno	*byehn, bwehnoh*
west	el oeste	*ehl ohehsteh*
wet	mojado	*mohahdoh*
wet (weather)	lluvioso	*lyoobyohsoh*
wetsuit	el traje de surf	*ehl trahheh deh soorf*
what?	¿qué?	*keh?*
wheel	la rueda	*lah rwehdah*
wheelchair	la silla de ruedas	*lah seelyah deh rwehdahs*
when?	¿cuándo?	*kwahndoh?*
where?	¿dónde?	*dohndeh?*
which?	¿cuál?	*kwahl?*
whipped cream	el chantilly	*ehl chahnteelyee*
whipping cream	la nata para batir	*lah nahtah pahrah bahteer*
white	blanco	*blahnkoh*
who?	¿quién?	*kyehn?*
wholemeal	integral	*eentehgrahl*
wholemeal bread	el pan integral	*ehl pahn eentehgrahl*
why?	¿por qué?	*pohr keh?*
wide-angle lens	el objetivo gran angular	*ehl obhehteeboh grahn ahngoolahr*
widow	la viuda	*lah byoodah*
widower	el viudo	*ehl byoodoh*
wife	la mujer	*lah moohehr*
wind	el viento	*ehl byehntoh*
windbreak	la protección contra el viento	*lah prohtehkthyohn kohntrah ehl byehntoh*
windmill	el molino	*ehl mohleenoh*
window	la ventanilla, la ventana	*lah behntahneelyah, lah behntahnah*

windscreen wiper	el limpiaparabrisas	*ehl leempyahpahrah-breesahs*
wine	el vino	*ehl beenoh*
wine list	la carta de vinos	*lah kahrtah deh beenohs*
winter	el invierno	*ehl eenbyehrnoh*
witness	el testigo	*ehl tehsteegoh*
woman	la mujer	*lah moo<u>h</u>ehr*
wood	la madera	*lah mahdehrah*
wool	la lana	*lah lahnah*
word	la palabra	*lah pahlahbrah*
work	el trabajo	*ehl trahbah<u>h</u>oh*
working day	el día laborable	*ehl deeah lahbohrahbleh*
worn/used	gastado	*gahstahdoh*
worried	inquieto	*eenkyehtoh*
wound	la herida	*lah ehreedah*
wrap (verb)	envolver	*ehnbohlbehr*
wrist	la muñeca	*lah moonyehkah*
write	escribir	*ehskreebeer*
write down	apuntar	*ahpoontahr*
writing pad	el bloc (cuadriculado, a rayas)	*ehl blohk(kwahdreekoo-lahdoh, ah rahyahs)*
writing paper	el papel de escribir	*ehl pahpehl deh ehskreebeer*
written	por carta	*pohr kahrtah*
wrong	mal, equivocado	*mahl, ehkeebohkahdoh*

Y

yacht	el yate	*ehl yahteh*
year	el año	*ehl anyoh*
yellow	amarillo	*ahmahreelyoh*
yes	sí	*see*
yes, please	con (mucho) gusto	*kohn (moochoh) goostoh*
yesterday	ayer	*ahyehr*
yoghurt	el yogur	*ehl yohgoor*
you (formal)	usted	*oostehd*
you too	igualmente	*eegwahlmehnteh*
youth hostel	el albergue juvenil	*ehl ahlbehrgueh <u>h</u>oobehneel*

Z

zip	la cremallera	*lah krehmahlyehrah*
zoo	el parque zoológico	*ehl pahrkeh thohohloh<u>h</u>eekoh*

Word list

15

Basic grammar

1 The article

Spanish nouns and adjectives are divided into 2 categories: masculine and feminine. The definite article (the) is **el** or **la**. Most masculine words end in **o** and most feminine words end in **a**.

el is used before masculine nouns, as in **el tren** (the train)
la is used before feminine nouns, as in **la playa** (the beach)
el is also used before feminine nouns beginning with a vowel, as in **el agua** (water).

Other examples are:

el techo	the roof	**la casa**	the house
el hambre	hunger	**el alma**	the soul

The plural of **el** is **los**; the plural of **la** is **las**.

In the case of the indefinite article (**a, an**):

un is used before masculine nouns, as in **un libro** (a book).

una is used before feminine nouns, as in **una mesa** (a table).

The plural is constructed by adding s, as in **unos camiones** (some lorries), **unas tazas** (some cups).

Other examples are:

un padre	a father	**una madre**	a mother
un hombre	a man	**una mujer**	a woman
unos hombres	men	**unas mujeres**	women

2 The plural

The plural of Spanish nouns and adjectives ends in **s**. Examples are:

singular	plural
el avión (the plane)	**los aviones**
la manzana (the apple)	**las manzanas**

3 Personal pronouns

I	**yo**
You	**tú/Usted**
He/she/it	**él/ella**
We	**nosotros/nosotras**
You	**vosotros/vosotras/Ustedes**
They	**ellos/ellas**

When speaking to a person one does not know well, **Usted** is used with the third person of the verb:

e.g. **Usted sabe/Ustedes saben**   you know

4 Possessive pronouns

	masculine/feminine	plural
my	**mi**	**mis**
your	**tu**	**tus**
his/her/its	**su**	**sus**
our	**nuestro/nuestra**	**nuestros/nuestras**
your	**vuestro/vuestra**	**vuestros/vuestras**
their	**su**	**sus**

They agree with the object they modify, e.g. our car = **nuestro coche**.

5 Verbs

Note: pronouns are only used with verbs when absolutely necessary.

hablar	to speak
hablo	I speak
hablas	you speak
habla	he/she/you speak
hablamos	we speak
habláis	you speak
hablan	they/you speak

Here are some useful verbs:

ser	**estar** (to be)
soy	**estoy**
eres	**estás**
es	**está**
somos	**estamos**
sois	**estáis**
son	**están**

Note: **estar** is used with places and also means a temporary state, e.g. **el hotel está en la plaza**, (the hotel is in the square), **la niña está cansada** (the little girl is tired).

tener (to have)	**hacer** (to do/make)
tengo	**hago**
tienes	**haces**
tiene	**hace**
tenemos	**hacemos**
tenéis	**hacéis**
tienen	**hacen**

ir (to go)	**ver** (to see)
voy	**veo**
vas	**ves**
va	**ve**
vamos	**vemos**
vais	**veis**
van	**ven**

Negatives are formed by putting no before the verb:
e.g. **no entiendo**, I do not understand; **no oigo**, I cannot hear.

6 Basic prepositions

a = to, e.g. **voy a Madrid, voy al mercado**.
en= in or at, e.g. **estoy en la tienda, estoy en casa**.